PRAISE FOR

THE BOOK DUDE'S GUIDE TO

SELF-PUBLISHING, BOOK 1:

THE MODERN AUTHOR

"Bro, this is awesome. Inspirational, informative, constructive, professional book. Reminds me of *Save The Cat!* where Blake Snyder takes writing screenplays and makes it easy to do. Like yours, easy steps to follow, not so scary, and all around a fun read. I read the entire book in a week. And your spirit is in this book, in the pages, words, letters, brother. Really great. One story where you came to a realization that it was ego leading you, really hit home. While reading, you were with us in this journey, not as a teacher or lecturer or boss, but as a guide, a mentor, a guru happily riding these waves of knowledge throughout the book! And I loved "Your Journey Is Sacred," those short but sweet points of life where you learn large lessons from small failures. Truly profound. There is no way I'd be where I am without you brother, I owe you a ton my friend. Thank you for sharing this with me, it's an honor and I really loved reading it bro!"

—DIONISIOS EFKARPIDIS,
AUTHOR, *DOGS OF CREATION*

"You give so much important information and even though I've been writing and ghostwriting books for years, I've never had a good understanding of all the self-publishing options, until now."

—CHRISTINA DEBUSK,
FREELANCE HEALTH WRITER

"This ... is ... awesome! Should be called the Indie Author Book Bible! I wish this was available when I started writing books, my life would have been so much more fun and stress-free! It is so easy to get lost and confused in the world of book creation that this is where most authors fail and their amazing ideas, stories, and creativity never get shared. It was Rodney who helped me not only create my first book series, he encouraged me to keep writing and to continually improve my work. Through to my latest multi-award-winning business book, Rodney has taken an increasing role in helping me shape and nurture my thought leadership to become a mighty resource that impacts thousands around the world. This is the power of having someone like Rodney, who lives and breathes books, by your side to assist you, the author, to create and deliver something extraordinary. What he doesn't know about book creation is not worth knowing and his patience and humble honesty is a godsend for any author. I am so grateful that Rodney has been by my side, not only as an author but as a business leader and keynote speaker. He has pushed me further than I thought possible and the books he has helped me create are having such an astounding impact on those around us, I know we have changed the course of many people's lives through our work together."

—LAUREN CLEMETT, AUTHOR,
FINDING YOUR BRAND TRUE NORTH

"I'm very impressed! So much information. Not only how to, but some clever tricks as well. For example, the "key word" suggestion. Honestly, it not only encourages a person to write but how to get their story out there the best possible way. Great job!"

—WAYNE CHASSON, AUTHOR,
THIS IS MINUTEMAN: TWO, THREE... GO!

"From cover to last page, your book exceeded all my ideas of what it would be. IT IS SOOOO YOU! I got lost in reading it, even more just to be in your easy conversational style and world than to learn about the specifics of book publishing. But I did read with that eye, and to me it was fantastic—great information presented in easy-to-understand writing, lots of personal voice and humor, and I could feel you wanted me to succeed."

—REVEREND MICHELLE HUBBARD, AUTHOR,
PERSONALIZE YOUR LAW SCHOOL ESSAYS

"I can unequivocally say that in the *Book Dude's Guide to Self-Publishing*, Rodney carefully and surgically strips the threads apart that constitute the self-publishing fabric, such that they are clearly made visible to the naked eye. Thank you Rodney, for epitomizing brilliance which is to explain complex things in simplistic fashion."

—ROBERT MULINDWA, AUTHOR,
CREATED FOR SUCCESS

"There is a saying that you shouldn't see 'how hotdogs are made.' But it was the complete opposite here. I love books, and it was quite interesting how they are made. Writing the book is just the first step of many. The prose was easy to read, and I really liked some of the anecdotes. Especially the one when the author gets valuable insight from the cashier. The anecdotes and the fun way of writing made the voice of the author very relatable, and it made me want to read more. It really felt like the author knew what they were saying. The amount of experience he had was coming off the pages. I really liked the modern meanings of regularly used literary terms. That was intriguing—words like "ignorance gap," and how shady publishers can trick naïve authors by using flashy yet self-serving words. The whole narrative here was quite engaging. I really had fun reading this and gaining new knowledge... I want to read the sequel! And I loved that the end felt very personal for the author. It genuinely felt like the author wants to help, and the knowledge and credentials proves that he can." —PRAGNA J.

"All in all, a fantastic experience. I thought I knew a lot in this field. I didn't. Learned a lot of new things and got inspired too. You can get your info from blogs or YouTube tutorials, but none will be as comprehensive and easy to understand as this book. I was on board right from the beginning. The language was easy to read and understand, the flow was great, and the content was personable and informative. I was engaged right to the end. It feels like I have accomplished something after reading this. There is a lot of information that is not just useful but crucial for most aspirational authors. And most of all, it was a fun experience reading the book."

—SIDD J., WRITER, EDITOR @SIDHARTHHJ,
HTTPS://WWW.FIVERR.COM/SIDHARTHHJ

THE BOOK DUDE'S GUIDE to SELF-PUBLISHING

Book 1

THE MODERN AUTHOR

By Rodney Miles Taber

—The Book Dude's Guide to Self-Publishing Series—
Book 1: The MODERN AUTHOR
Book 2: The BOOK CREATION CYCLE (2023)
Book 3: EXPONENTIAL AUTHOR GROWTH (2024)

—The Inspiring Women Today Series—
Inspiring Women Today, Volume 1
Inspiring Women Today, Volume 2 (2023)
Inspiring Women Today, Volume 3 (2024)

365 Surprising and Inspirational Rock Star Quotes
by Rodney Miles and Alison Taylor

All You Need is Love: Real Stories of Kindness
compiled by Rodney Miles

THE BOOK DUDE'S GUIDE

to SELF-PUBLISHING

Book 1

THE MODERN AUTHOR

Bringing you up-to-date on the DRASTIC CHANGES in publishing, aware of opportunities and immune to pitfalls, making YOU a smart, modern author.

RODNEY MILES

RM
RODNEY MILES
Creating Successful Books & Authors

For the Great Library.

thebookdude.com
SELF-PUBLISHING EDUCATION

"Nothing will ever please me,
no matter how excellent or beneficial,
if I must keep the knowledge of it
to myself…
No good thing is pleasant to possess
without friends to share it."

—SENECA, *LETTERS 6.4*

NOTE TO READERS

THROUGHOUT THIS BOOK I mention certain books and projects I am very proud to have been a part of in some way, and that's not to prove what I've worked on but in the hopes of supporting these authors and their great books, to provide actual examples, and to give this book a bit of color at the same time. Please check them out! Whenever possible I link to the author's website or retail book page. You can also visit my website and see many more titles I've gotten to work on in some way. I really want to do what I can to support the authors who have trusted me with their projects and taught me so much.

In the back of the book there are several pages of additional "Praise" to show that what I'm about to share really works. And frankly, after 13 years, it's been a profound thrill to reflect on all of this.

And finally, in the *very back* of this book I now have a list of abbreviations for easy reference. Beta reader feedback showed this (all the abbreviations) to be an issue—I get tired of writing full names out, I guess, and take for granted that readers know what I'm talking about! I hope it makes things easier.

Thank you!

CONTENTS (BRIEF)

Contents (Expanded)

FOREWORD

BY LAUREN CLEMETT

WELCOME to the exhilarating (and exhausting) world of self-publishing! In the vast landscape of literature, one thing remains constant: the deep desire within each of us to share our stories, experiences, and wisdom with the world. Once we know we want to publish a book, it becomes a constantly nagging feeling that resonates deep within our souls, an unyielding whisper that our book needs to be written.

But here's the thing, as T.S. Eliot so eloquently put it…

> "Between the idea and reality,
> lies the shadow."

While everyone may have a book in them, not everyone can find their way through the minefield of publishing to realise their dream. As someone immersed in the overwhelming world of self-publishing since 2012, I've seen countless aspiring authors grapple with the daunting task of transforming their ideas into a real live book. Overwhelmed by the complexity of the process, they sadly resign themselves to the belief that their work may never see the light of day.

Worse, many get to publish their book, often investing huge time and money into the process only to end up with boxes of books gathering dust in the garage.

Enter Rodney Miles, writer, editor, publisher, and most importantly, a true friend. Rodney has made it his life's mission to empower others like you to overcome the obstacles of becoming an author, bringing your literary dreams to fruition. With his wisdom, dedication, and expertise, he has not only transformed manuscripts but also transformed lives.

In the pages that follow, you will discover a treasure trove of knowledge meticulously crafted by Rodney. This book is nothing short of a Bible for authors seeking to navigate the mystical labyrinth of self-publishing. It is a roadmap to success, an indispensable guide that demystifies the publishing process and equips you with the tools to not only write your book but to publish it with ease (and more!).

Rodney's approach has always been a breath of fresh air in an industry that can often feel intimidating and exclusive. He understands the trials and tribulations that authors face because he's been there himself and worked with so many of us from all walks of life. His empathetic, patient, and encouraging style will not only help you overcome your fear but also guide you through the intricacies of editing, formatting, creating, and marketing your work.

As you delve into the pages of this book (the first in his series), you will find yourself not just learning, but growing as an author. Rodney doesn't simply provide knowledge; he nurtures your creativity, fosters your confidence, and ignites your passion for writing.

So, intrepid reader, whether you're a seasoned writer or someone who's just beginning to explore the world of words, know that you hold in your hands the key to unlocking your authorial potential. Rodney Miles is your mentor, your confidant, and your guide on this incredible journey. With his guidance, you too can take your literary aspirations and transform them into reality.

Prepare to embark on a transformative voyage, for within these pages lies the wisdom that will enable you to shine as an author. Your story deserves to be told, your words deserve to be read, and Rodney Miles is here to help you make that dream come alive.

Congratulations on taking the first step towards becoming a published author. May your journey be as enriching and fulfilling as the words you are about to create.

—LAUREN CLEMETT

Dyslexic Award-Winning Author of Best-Selling Books

https://www.linkedin.com/in/laurenclemett/

PREFACE

"The advancement and diffusion of
knowledge is the only guardian
of true liberty."

—JAMES MADISON

THIS BOOK took thirteen years to write. That doesn't mean
it's great, nor that it sucks, but only that I've been through
whatever you're going through in your own dream of being an
author, and that I'm now an expert in the fields of both
procrastination and self-publishing. When I started
ghostwriting for a penny a word, I knew little and got excited
a lot. *I was in books!* And as soon as I felt my feet planted in
the business, I wanted to write a book about writing books.
But as with the cobbler's kids, I always seemed too busy (a
good thing, for a writer), or life got in the way, or I had not
yet perfected the expertise to include in such a book, yet.

Every now and then I'd sit down between projects for
others (and on occasion of my own) and make a little progress,
and the book you now hold started to evolve. I originally
called it *My Romance with Elance,* because I started writing for-
hire with that online freelancer platform (Elance, which today
is called Upwork). I'd make a note or write a few pages or draw

an outline or even record ideas into a little hand recorder, stopping the lawn mower to do so. After all, I had learned to coach other (usually first-time) authors to create their content in whatever way served them best, and the material for this book (series) grew in fits and starts, saw several concept and cover designs and changes, and after copying and pasting what I thought were tasty bits of wisdom here and there through the years, swelled to a 389,000-word sort of Frankenstein of a file.

I finally started taking my own advice. I started cutting more than pasting. I wanted a *tight* but readable book, if I could manage it, with a good *value* for readers, and I wanted to share what I learned in the wonderful career I still love. I mean, you're my compadres, you're possibly a *bibliophile* or a lover of reading, like me. You either dream (privately or openly) of being an author, penning a memoir or poems, fiction, or how-to. Maybe a book is the catalyst to a new or re-invigorated career for you. Maybe, as a few of my clients have done, you want to start a publishing imprint/house of your own. In the very least, you see the value in creating a worthy book, for whatever reason important or even sacred *to you*. And no matter what you think of this book, because you're now holding it, *I like you*. And *I'm so glad I finally did it, and you will be, too*.

See, the more worthy books there are, the better.

THE GREAT LIBRARY

When you add your book to the world you are adding your thought, experience, ideas, even your emotion—love, hate, whatever—to what I call The Great Library—all the *books in their various modern forms* available to a civilization. The more sincere thought available to us, the better it is for all of us.

What will you add to The Great Library?

> "I've never met an author that was sorry he or she wrote their book. They were only sorry they did not write it sooner."
>
> — SAM HORN

And again, after a *wonderful* career helping others write, edit, design, and publish their books, I've finally written mine. I hope this book series helps and inspires you to get your own book(s) done and done like the pros, so you can take that next step you've been dreaming of, and be happy with it all your life.

Please reach out and tell me when you do!

—RODNEY MILES TABER
rmiles@rodneymiles.com
September 2023
Cape Canaveral, Florida

THE MODERN AUTHOR

"The fundamental cause of the trouble
is that in the modern world
the stupid are cocksure while the
intelligent are full of doubt."

— BERTRAND RUSSELL

THIS BOOK SERIES touches on every significant step or idea I can think of that comprise "best practices" in self-publishing, but please keep in mind:

- You can but don't have to do them all, in fact a plan tailored to your goals, time, and budget with an eye to your bigger picture is what you *should* do, and...

- I can't possibly dive as deep as every point goes, nor into every nook and cranny of what can happen, as wide as that goes. In fact, things are constantly changing—publishing options, Amazon policies, software, you name it.

- As with seemingly all books on self-publishing, I, the author, stress you take away *evergreen principles* regardless of current methods, names, and platforms.

Knowing how things were done in the past can help you understand the present. Through my career I've tried to stay abreast of things but I've also been very interested in the "old ways." For example, it seems traditional publishers in the past when releasing a book for a big name author would only release a hardcover and make you wait a full year for the paperback. Observing that, we might connect the dots and think that was (A) to concentrate sales for the *New York Times Best Seller List* which used to focus on hardcovers, and (B) perhaps for better margins that first year, given cost-effective print runs. (Hardcover is still a hard nut to crack for indies due to costs.)

Today we find some things remain exactly as they were, some only remain in some form, and some have completely changed. And simply, knowing that makes us *modern authors,* professionals who understand *function* as well as form. And guess how, in large, I've found so much of this out? ... Books!

And so, the principles in this book series evolved from long-established *traditional and self-publishing best practices*, and they will guide you to an outstanding book, maybe even get you to a dream career as an author or publisher—a career you might not yet think possible (but it is).

I get up each day around 9 or 10 a.m., make my wife and me a nice casual breakfast, get a few work tasks completed and my plan made for the workday. Then we walk or ride to the beach (most days). If we're lucky we swim or surf and walk, then head back, clean up, start work again from our RV, take a break to cook a nice meal (maybe stuffed shrimp or something), then dive down a rabbit hole or two on author-client projects or my own books. We think we invented a drink we call a "Jetty Cooler" (lemonade, Malibu, KeKe Key Lime Liquor, and a splash of Siesta Key Toasted Coconut Rum), but we don't always drink, even though I'm a writer.

And that's a fairly typical workday. I'm not rich, but we're happy and we're *free.* And I love what I do. We live two blocks from the beach and my own books are starting to grow into something, with the idea of researching, writing, and publishing more of *what I find important* as my "end game." We seem to have *enough.* Which brings us to the book cover. You'd think I'd have a stack of books or a humungous pencil or something, maybe Daffy Duck throwing money in the air, or even images from a professional photo shoot, but I'm not after any of those things.

I write and publish because I love it and believe books make a difference. And luckily, people pay me to help them do that, too. And further, nobody really wants a drill, they want holes, so me sitting on the beach while I get distracted by a coastline full of sparkles and hues of blues is one reward I really appreciate, and it's a lifestyle available to you (or whatever your Shangri-La might be), with enough books and enough readers, of course.

You can have a life as an author, or in freelancing, writing, or publishing. With a book or books you can leave a legacy or create, enhance, or memorialize a career.

After thirteen years of writing, editing, publishing, and working with author-clients, I've learned the business. Book 1 in this series, *The Modern Author,* brings you up to speed on the industry as it is now versus where it has been in the past. It reveals a few secrets and exploited misunderstandings that will save you time, effort, even embarrassment, so your book project as well as your finished book are the best they can be and just as important, accomplish your goal(s). It explains platforms, procedures, and the publishing industry as it was when I started and as it is today. It lays out those things I typically explain in an intro call with a new client as they are diving into creating a book for the first time. It's about being *safe and savvy.*

In my career I've devised, initially for my own use, what I call the "Book Creation Cycle," which I explain in this first book and much more fully in the next, *The Book Dude's Guide to Self-Publishing, Book 2: The Book Creation Cycle.* The "cycle" lays out the meat and potatoes of any successful book project. You should do all of the possible steps of that cycle but you don't have to, of course. It all depends on your goals, time, resources, and budget, but you should be aware of what your options and opportunities are. Again, it's all about *best practices.*

Book 3, Exponential Growth, is about more than "book sales," it's about out-of-the-box solutions to becoming a full-time author faster, or booming a publishing house, or making the most of your book for credibility, legacy, and profit. The idea of *exponential growth* I learned from editing Nick Bradley's awesome book about private equity, *Exit for Millions.* (I've received a whole education from my clients, from organic health to project management to you name it.) When you do all the things authors seem to do—build your backlist of books, place ads, create a website, make appearances, build an email list of readers—these are *organic growth,* and there are ample books, blogs, and podcasts out there on these things. *Strategic growth* is using *strategies* such as partnerships, mergers, acquisitions, and leverage to grow. When you combine the two, organic and strategic growth, you get *exponential growth,* the like of which is typically enjoyed by private equity and other big shots, and I thought I'd research and see how this might be applied to authors, and of course, write a book about it.

There are now over *one million* new books published every year, so the ideas in this book series are intended to help raise your own drop in the ocean (your book) to the very top, along with your career as an author or otherwise.

What's perhaps different about this book series is that almost all of the books on self-publishing I've found and read and valued over the years were written by *authors*. Well, I'm an author, myself, but more than that I'm a *service industry professional*, having specialized these many years in *production* (planning, writing, editing, design, publishing).

I think you should read us both.

In another life, I was a member of a rather large church. There was a thing going on where many of us were making donations, and I visited the "registrar," or the dude who took your money and gave you a receipt. I made my rather modest donation and as he was writing me a receipt, Paul (the dude) asked me, "So, what are you doing these days?"

I assumed he meant for work, so I said, with my chest puffed, "Rehabbing, flipping houses." He nodded and kept at the bookkeeping. I was young, excited, proud, and I continued, "I've done a few smaller ones in St. Pete, but I'm working on doing larger, nicer homes."

"Nah, you don't want to do that," he said with a wave of his hand, not even looking up at me.

I was insulted. *How dare he? Who the hell is this guy, anyway? He's not out there doing it. He sits here and counts money. What the hell does he know about flipping houses?*

"I don't?" I asked.

"Nope."

So certain is he!

"Why is that Paul?"

He stopped counting and looked me in the eye. "Rodney, I sit here and work with *hundreds* of people in the community, and a lot of them are doing what you do. The guys doing big houses are losing their asses, and the guys who are doing the little houses are making steady donations. Keep with the small houses, and we'll both be fine."

It was a moment of truth (one of many) where I was lucky enough in life to *see* that *my ego* was leading me, not common sense. *Holy shit,* I realized, *No one knows more about flipping houses than Paul! He sits here all day and listens to how the many house-flippers are doing, and further, he knows how well they're doing, and he can probably figure out why or why not.*

I walked out of there probably looking like Moses as he descended that mountain with those tablets.

Years later, my accountant, who always seemed miserable, revealed, "Oh I *love* what I do."

"You do?" I said.

"Yes, I do. I get to see inside of all these fascinating businesses."

Again, I was blown away.

I think we learn best by experience, and if we're really smart, we learn by *someone else's experience.* This book series is based on thirteen years of my experience, work, trial and error, study, failure (we might learn most from failure), and success. And I bet we all define "success" a bit differently.

So, I have something to offer. And I know that *you do,* too. In fact, I've found...

We usually don't know how much we know
until we try to teach it or write about it.

You know more than you think you know. You are a special,
three-dimensional person, with a story that matters to someone.
Now, you can share that, learn from it, and help someone.

That's part of the joy, whether writing a book, teaching, or parenting. And as teachers, parents—as anyone who wants to share anything at all and have it received—*we have a duty to share it in its most interesting way.* That's why they make movies about teachers who care enough to step outside of boxes.

I think you should do what you're passionate about. There was a time when we all needed to be either farmers or soldiers, but that's not the case today. Today, I believe we have a moral imperative to find our own highest and best use. And that's usually what we're passionate about. So in this book series we'll happily address not only *why* you want to write and publish a book (or books), but also *how.* Part of these best practices is defining "success," not only for your book but for *you.* Don't worry, we'll be quick, but promise me you'll take your time as we go.

"Slow is smooth, smooth is fast."

— NAVY SEAL SAYING

In this series, in Book 1, these are the modern understandings that will make your book project a success. In Book 2, these are the steps that will make your book accepted and successful. And with Book 3, you can build a firm foundation and expand or scale *quickly.*

If you have a breakdown of what it takes to *professionally* create a book—the writing, editing, design, production, distribution, launch, marketing, and building author platforms—you can plan, you can create a project, and you can do well. You can plan your book project over a few months or a year, and you can plan and do it all yourself, if you choose to. Or you can build a team, small or large. Or you can make it your business. Everything I'm about to share with you was designed to make the process easy for me and for my clients, in particular clients without a lot of time to create their books. It was designed to be fun, and designed to make things smooth in hopes of encouraging nice epiphanies along the way, no matter how experienced or smart we think we are already in our own fields.

And if you are thinking of making this a career, I hope this gets you started. They say most books sell less than 200 copies, and the majority of those copies are bought by the author. That's not what I want for you! If we step back a bit we can first define "success" for *you* and for your book, and in the process take your book from an idea, to reality, to *healthy,* make it *good* and maybe even *great,* then *seasoned* and *successful.* Nothing is more motivating than results, but we need to define these terms first, and we do that here, in this first book.

I have great respect for people who come from both self-publishing and traditional publishing and share what they know so the industry can improve. It's going on all around us. New models for publishing are springing up and evolving all the time, but I find the best practices that make a book the best it can be seem to remain the same, and for that, you will now have the modern concepts that define a *modern author,* you'll have the Book Creation Cycle, and you'll have effective strategies for growth. For everything else, I hope you're about to be encouraged.

THE BOOK DUDE

Under A 20' by 20' outdoor event tent at the Wisconsin State Fair in 2010, on a wet (but not raining) day, my best friend Lloyd was giving a live cookware demonstration to about 40 people. His voice flowed over the PA as laughter filled the audience here and there. I knew the script, I'd done it myself for a while. I was there now helping Lloyd, both to earn a few bucks and to try and get some of my writing going. I was 40 years old and had, a few years earlier, left real estate brokerage after the bubble burst in Florida (and everywhere else). I was reinventing myself, this time in what I'd earlier dreamed of for my life, a life of writing books... hopefully.

Behind the curtain backdrop of his display, there was about a two-foot-wide space between that curtain and the back wall of the tent. It was skinny storage space, holding the PA equipment, black cases of cookware, and piles of cases of bottled water. I'd arranged a folding chair and a power strip so I could carefully sit there (sideways) and type into my laptop, with an ear for any indication Lloyd might need me in some way.

It struck me that the job I'd bid on (and won) with Elance was not going to work, because if I did complete it, it might ruin me. I was living thrifty, with pressure to figure out how to make more money with writing *fast,* or find a job. A real job. But on this one, only after winning and starting into it did I calculate it would take tens of hours and tons of research to write something like *100 articles* on meditation. Delirium tremens. That sick feeling. But then clarity. I was brand-new to Elance and reviews meant everything. I started typing, and explained to my client I simply could not, for personal reasons, continue with the project, but the articles I had written were now his *for free*, and because this was surely a setback for him (my bowing out), I was refunding the project fee *and also sending him $50* as some small compensation for the confusion.

He thanked me and left a great review.

About a year later I had a handful of regular clients. For one in particular I had been writing a lot of books, about a small book every week of about 25,000 words of researched non-fiction (much harder than 25,000 words of fiction). I had developed by then two methods for writing these books of expertise quickly, either "top-down" with an outline, or "bottom up" going wherever the research led me, sometimes both. They (a small publishing partnership in Australia) liked what I wrote and started asking me to write more, and to look over what other writers had been turning in and fixing those, if I could. Soon they asked me to hire and oversee writers, and to handle all of the editing, design, and production of files. They would handle the uploads to Kindle and CreateSpace.

I came to understand I was actually an *editor-in-chief.* I was managing the writing department and managing writers. I did developmental editing and hired out the copy editing. I would try to get as clear a mandate as possible from the author-client, pick a writer who seemed appropriate, and have them send me small chunks of writing for me to approve or instruct upon, edit, and send to the client for review, to make sure we were on track and they liked the writing and so forth. We started slowly, *carefully*, but were soon able to move forward *confidently*.

My little writing department grew and I was having a blast. We had about 25 freelance writers, an editor, and a cover designer. I learned the value of a great assistant as a real estate broker, and hired Jessica to help me with everything, and she was amazing.

I miss those days.

The Australian partnership fell apart but they graciously sent a few remaining clients to me, to be the first author-clients I would work with directly and more deeply in their projects. *Larger more serious books.* I was thrilled, actually. Cynthia Freeman, author of *The Power of Done,* and Erin Mahoney, author of *Girl Power* were two of the very first. I love them both, and their books, to this day. And these were not ghostwritten as so many back then were. I decided I needed some kind of name credit to build a portfolio and so became a "collaborator." We created a lot of their content from transcribed interviews, notes, and research.

I sat back at that point and realized I had helped create probably in the area of 150 short (12,000- to 30,000-word) books of expertise, some autobiographical. I'd written 50 myself, and overseen and edited and produced probably another 100. We did 13 in one week, I remember. But now the larger fees and ability to dive deeper one-on-one with author-clients was *wonderful.* I again cut my teeth on *lots of work.* I read blogs and books about both self- and traditional publishing, and followed self-published authors like David Gaughran, Joanna Penn, and Derek Murphy. I learned industry history and kept up on industry news. I started a small publishing house (Bimini Books) for the purpose of learning publishing more directly, and hired some of the writers we had on the team (freelancers from all over the world) to create short, "lifestyle" books I could edit, design, and publish, to better learn the process.

I loved every minute of it.

Meanwhile Jessica and I had grown fond of an old-time traditional publisher out on his own named Sean, and the three of us briefly formed a small publishing house—*an actual publishing house.* Sean had a wealth of wisdom from traditional publishing, the three of us got along great, and for a while we had a blast. Among the writers we scouted and talked to, a gifted fantasy writer named Sally had a following of 26,000 readers on Wattpad with over *2 million* reads. We "signed her" and launched her first fantasy novel as *publishers*. Wattpad, where she had established herself, is a free reading platform, so those 26,000 readers were not necessarily going to translate directly into sales, but it felt like a great start! I designed her book cover and looked to other tasks, always learning from Sean.

I actually left that small *hybrid* publishing house because I realized my role—despite the title of CEO—had very little autonomy (at least in our case). Sean, the editor-in-chief, was the real creative, strategic, force among us, while "CEO" was to be the person who handled all of the legal and administrative stuff. *Blecch.* It was hard to leave, but *good is the enemy of great,* and that CEO role was not what I got into writing for!

I was back on my own again, and I liked it. I was doing full collaboration projects for $5,000 that included writing, editing, design, production, distribution, and the basics of launch, marketing, and building author platforms. This first sequence of steps was the start of what I now call the Book Creation Cycle, now with many refinements and additions, but I learned the basics through those initial years, through lots of work, and by the grace of so many others. I helped create about 12 books each year, and what my clients never saw was how feast and famine for me (and my family) the whole thing was. *But I loved every minute, even those few occasions, out of hundreds, where there was a disagreement. In fact I learned even more from those few than expected, both business-wise and personally.*

After many years of collaborations, I went back to online freelancing to see if I could pick up worthwhile smaller projects. Besides, I was eager to *finally* write and publish more of my own work. This is when *Inspiring Women Today* was conceived. I hoped less commitment with fewer larger projects might afford me more time for my own work. Elance had now become Upwork, so I built a portfolio there (again) and have not looked back. I've been very pleasantly surprised at the quality of projects, excellence of the platform, and wonderful clients I've met on Upwork.

I worked myself up to $100 per hour, and highly recommend Upwork and online freelancing. In fact, by now I've been lucky enough to have been invited and participated in beta programs with both Kindle Direct Publishing as well as Upwork, and hope to one day lay this out in detail in an upcoming book, perhaps *The Book Dude's Guide to Successful Freelancing,* we'll see. The experience has made me see freelancing with online platforms not as a stepping stone (as I used to see it), but as a safe place where anyone with sincere work and good strategy can build a *wonderful* freelancing career, full of colorful clients, plenty of moolah if managed well, and most of all, *freedom.*

> *The way you get out of the system*
> *is not by slaving away your whole life*
> *for enough "wealth" to buy your way out,*
> *but just by stepping out of it*
> *and focusing on "real" wealth.*

Read the "Mexican fisherman story" in *The Four-Hour Work Week* by Tim Ferris, for example. The gist is a wealthy, overworked lawyer from the U.S. vacations in Mexico and is out on a small fishing boat with a local guide. He's having such a great, relaxing time, he says to the guide, "Say, why don't you sock away a little money and buy another fishing boat?"

"Why?" asks the guide.

"So you can double your gross profit," says the attorney.

"Why?" asks the guide.

"Well, so you can buy even more fishing boats," says the attorney.

"Why?" asks the guide.

"So, of course, with a small fleet, you can make a whole lot more money," says the attorney.

"Why?" asks the guide.

"So one day if you work hard and long enough, years from now you might retire and be able to spend more time alone on a small ... fishing ... boat." He almost stopped himself.

The guide smiled, and must have wondered why rich Americans drive themselves so crazy.

Today, my daughter has moved on and my wife and I RV fulltime by the beach. We travel whenever we can. I work on my own schedule, love my clients, and make $100 per hour from my laptop. I have not placed a bid on a project in years, and fortunately get invited to many. We "beach" all the time and I get to surf sometimes. Every client and every book project *is special, and I want them all to love their books. Simple.* It's a great life, "author, publisher, consultant." And I'm ready to share what I've found and hopefully encourage more people now through this book series, my podcast, and perhaps masterminds and retreats (in Cocoa Beach, of course).

This first book is the "wax on, wax off" part of your training. After we discuss key concepts and changes in the industry, you should be happy to find you can defend yourself and make strides with clarity and understanding in your writing and publishing. Heck, you might find yourself explaining these things to others.

BOOKS, BOOKS, BOOKS

I can tell quickly how well-read a client is, and even what they probably like to read. That's because *we write as we read.* It's amazing, actually, I tested it myself once. I was writing regularly and son of a gun if while I was reading Erik Larsen I didn't write *like* Erik Larsen, or as I read Hemingway I didn't write *like* Hemingway. I don't mean *as well as* in either case, but *like*. It's actually a pro tip:

> *Try not to change authors you're reading*
> *too often during a writing period of a*
> *single work.*

It's so much the case you can test it yourself, as I did and found my writing style changed after I switched what I was reading.

And if we can back up just a tad, let me place the greatest tip of all right here:

> *The best way to become a great writer*
> *is read and write a lot.*

Notice, there's no "go to college," no "join a local writer's group," no "study the craft," and so on. Read and write a lot. *So many famous writers recommend exactly this!* All those other things have a place, I'll even recommend a few, but the above tip, if you did only *one thing* (okay, maybe two things), *read and write a lot.* Some clients don't. Some just want a book to boost their business or commit their life to posterity—all good, of course. But the above tip stands for those of you who want to dive into the craft, and it's not even my tip—it's again, a consensus among many a famous writer.

For example…

> "I have quite a few friends who are writers, and most of them believe that the creation of well-crafted fiction cannot be taught… by attending creative writing classes or by reading textbooks… I agree. To a certain extent, a novel can be dissected… but a pathologist cannot find a man's soul while doing an autopsy… Primarily, one learns to write fiction by writing it, then by writing more of it and more of it and more…"
>
> —DEAN KOONTZ,
> *How to Write Best Selling Fiction* (1981)

I was writing a lot for myself over an intense period, joyfully, and developed a piece of advice I then shared with an author-client. He had, later in life, re-discovered poetry and was, joyfully, running with it, himself. So, I told him:

> *Once you've written about 100,000 words*
> *you really start to find your own voice.*

He agreed, and he was excited, because he was finding his own voice, and it was wonderful to him!

And this is not by any means bad news. It means it doesn't matter what that "teacher" who makes you feel unsure about your talent says, or the publisher who ignores or rejects your submission, or your friend who rather than simply validate what you share, offers advice and alternatives (which can serve to fracture you if you're still unsure of yourself). Writing is not "agony" as the *literate elites* would like you to think. Working on roofs, resurfacing pools, spiritual atrophy in a cubicle, those are "agony." Sitting in front of a typewriter or computer and "bleeding," as Hemingway would say, or researching, compared to other professions, these are *gifts and opportunities from God not to be squandered.*

Did I, do I read and write a lot? Probably, yes. On writing, I don't write nearly as much as I want for myself because I am still a provider of "author services and self-publishing consulting." I write for others… a lot. On reading, it's hard to say actually because most *bibliophiles* (and I am one) feel they don't read enough, and never do, never can, perhaps. See, with books, the world and beyond is at your fingertips. I can say that I find reading and writing *insatiable.* In fact, *any subject you want thought on can usually be found in books,* even more so than from movies and other media, each which has its plusses. With books I have independently advanced my thinking and understanding on so many things.

I remember being probably seven years old watching my mom drive us around Staten Island. At stop signs and red lights she'd often break open a book and read a few pages. At home, her book collection was neatly shelved everywhere. She prized two custom-made white adjustable bookshelves that ran floor-to-ceiling. I commonly saw author names such as James Michener, Alex Haley, Stephen King, Danielle Steele, Sidney Sheldon, Ken Follet, as well as a beautiful set of *World Book* encyclopedias and books on all kinds of subjects like space, animals, cooking, and so much more.

I used to save my change I gathered cleaning out the washers and dryers in our apartment complex so I could go to Paul's corner store and buy *MAD Magazine* and order paperbacks by my favorite MAD guys like Sergio Aragonés, Don Martin, and Al Jaffee. I'd place cash, sometimes exact change, in an envelope and mail it to MAD Magazine headquarters in Manhattan, and they'd send me my prize paperbacks. And when I wasn't allowed to go see *The Exorcist* in theaters, I read Mom's book (so much better than the movie, and based on non-fiction, believe it or not).

In my teens I found books on sex… and read them. Heck, I almost called this book *The Joy of Books*. And from twelve to this day I *read* on spirituality, history, and so on. Growing up in Lutheran schools centered around study of *the Book, The Bible,* and through high school and college, ironically, I read everything I could get my hands on *except* what was "required." (*Forcing* students to read books is a great way to ruin any love of reading they might have had, but more on pedagogy in other places.)

Books are a unique and magical way to immerse yourself in another's life, in subject matter, in other times and places, and other worlds. They offer a much deeper and more thorough delving than do movies and film, and per square hour, offer much more than many classes and courses, all at one's own pace and pleasure. They also do more to *engage the imagination* than visual media.

And books are cheap, often free. Libraries are *important cultural resources.* Amazon has crushed bookstores, which sucks, but bookstores seem to be making a comeback—small ones, anyway, and I have mostly good things to say about Amazon. But come on—for $12 you can spend three or four hours with an expert—seriously? And have all that info preserved and readily accessible right in your library, car, or bathroom? Or for $2.99 you can escape from time-to-time to a world of fantasy and adventure? Or for $24.99 you can gaze upon big, sweeping views of exotic places right on your coffee table?

Books are *miracles.* Just imagine the leap to literacy, where standing around in furry caveman shorts (if that's how it actually went) someone says, "No go that-a-way, big bear! Go this-a-away!" Boy, did that little piece of telepathy just save us not only a lot of time, but our very lives! We've now made another leap perhaps, from "literacy" to "electracy[1]," and my, how digital media has changed the landscape!

One hundred years from now someone can pick up your book and read it, and if done well, they can experience *you*— your tone, your spirit, your intellect—as if you are right there with them. A miracle, really. Hey, right now I'm talking to *you,* right?

Books are special:

- You can see this world and others, and you can live a thousand lives, real or imagined, with books.

- Reading books gives a sense of accomplishment (and small wins count as much neurologically as large wins, according to some).

- Books engage and spark your imagination.

- Books share intelligence, philosophy, and emotional experience.

- Books can change and expand your mind and your world view.

---

[1] See https://en.wikipedia.org/wiki/Electracy and thanks to Professor Ulmer who enthralled me as a 40-year-old college student (the best age to go to college, actually).

- Books and study trigger new neural connections in the brain. (I *will not* be citing and trying to prove too much to you in these books, but I encourage us all to dig and do our own research with the rabbit holes we choose.)

- Books can provide intimately experienced memories, even if you've never been there (which was Hemingway's goal for his writing, and as such he relied a great deal on memory, killing himself when it faded).

- Books develop creative and critical thinking.

- They often offer remedies and catharsis.

- I'll bet they raise intelligence.

- They facilitate focus and relaxation…

- Engagement

- Enlightenment

- Skills and knowledge

- New ideas

- Affirmations

- Escape.

All great, right? But what do they mean for the self-publisher? It depends on what type of author you are.

AUTHOR, AUTHOR!

I divide author-clients into categories, each with different goals, although they often overlap:

- The **Expert**

- The **Legacy** or **Visionary** (for example, a dad who creates a children's book from his nighttime story to his child, or anyone who creates a book as part of a dream they've had, whether a children's book or otherwise)

- The **Memoirist** or **Autobiographer**

- The **Professional Author**

THE EXPERT

In my practice, the Expert is the most prevalent because these are usually businesspeople who see their book as an investment with a hoped-for return and they hire author services. When I started, this was the type of author we worked with exclusively in the Australian partnership because they were buying a marketing package that included publishing a book. And I still love working on business books, with several in-progress, even today.

Still—and I'll always be grateful for these experiences—the subjects covered vary from project management to organic gardening, team building, clean water, even adult coloring books (which when therapeutic are certainly "books of expertise[2]"), you name it. Wonderful experience. And these include, of course, books on self-development and coaching[3], and even with a religious focus[4].

Today, *books of expertise* is still an extremely popular niche for small and other publishers because authors make money on things *other than* book sales and can recoup their investment, often in the tens of thousands of dollars, with a single new client as the result of a book, or they raise rates, or launch speaking and consulting careers.

THE LEGACY OR VISIONARY

These authors are always fulfilling to work with, though fewer in number, because what they are memorializing is always special, whether simply for them (to publish a children's book, for example), or for a few, if not many. These authors, in fact, make it clear to me what a privilege it is to do what I do. For examples:

---

[2] Check out Reverend Michelle Hubbard and her therapeutic adult coloring book, *ScaredNSacred*

[3] *This is Coaching: How to Transform a Client's Performance, Life & Business as a Master Coach & Warrior of Love* by Matt Thieleman

[4] *Created for Success: Finding God's Will, Our Purpose, and True Happiness* by Robert Mulindwa

- I've had the pleasure of interviewing several generations and putting together a narrative in a *family legacy book.*

- I've helped create and publish several books for families who have suffered or survived a tragedy and want to share that experience with others who might be in the same place.

- We've memorialized nighttime stories and family traditions, even psychological lessons for children in children's books.

- And so much more.

THE MEMOIRIST OR AUTOBIOGRAPHER

I have a special passion for biographies—in fact I've been a fan of biographies and memoirs since long before being a writer/publisher. As they say,

A person is a story.

Those who are aware their story has something important to share are *inward- and outward-looking, courageous* people. I know how much I've learned from them and their books. I've gotten to work with courageous memoirists who not only memorialize their lives or experiences in books, but include very personal and profound subjects such as a missing[5] or the loss[6] of a child, religious books that are also memoirs[7], and books that teach us about other important subjects like surviving life with a narcissist[8], or beating cancer[9].

I've found the *process* of writing a business book advances your expertise because you examine what you know, organize it, realize relative importances, and then make it all assimilable for others. This happens in almost every expert project, and at all levels. We even coin new (often proprietary) terms and procedures in the process. I found the same happens in creating a memoir or autobiography, but rather than improved intelligence and practices, an author-client reaches new *understandings* and even *catharsis*. Amazing.

THE PROFESSIONAL AUTHOR

Of late, the professional author has my special interest, perhaps because I am myself transitioning into one by cherry-picking collaboration projects and spending more time creating and publishing my own books. I'm also about to fully engage on research into jump-starting an author career with selling books directly (for better margins and control) and with more *strategic ways* in addition to traditional (organic) ways, as stated, for *exponential growth*. And for so many, writing and publishing a book is no less than a dream, a life

---

[5] *Missing Sarah Pryor: A Mother's Testimony of Choosing Love over Grief and Emptiness* by Barbara Prior

[6] *When God Gives a Gift: In Memoriam of Layke Huxton Miller, 2019 - 2020* by Taylor & Candace Miller

[7] *The Hurricane Within* by Ashlee Leppert

[8] *I Loved You More* by Regina Rossi

[9] *Ganbaru Mindset: Do Your Best: Successful Mind Management Through Brain Cancer* by Luke Amery

event. How cool then, to work with a gifted author to develop and grow their *author career!*

"Professional author" here does not necessarily mean you *are* a full-time author… yet, but that it's your goal, which then informs what we do (methodically build a backlist of books, author infrastructure, and so on). And it's a blast! I am currently working with a half-dozen authors who are building to live their lives *as authors.*

Each author type will have slightly different paths and destinations, but from the top of that short list to the bottom, we move from a focus on credibility to a long-term approach to book sales. See, all projects consist of:

1. Time

2. Scope

3. Budget

So we take into account one's goals, hopes, and dreams, and weigh those against one's resources (time, energy, money), and plan our projects accordingly.

But anyone today can self-publish their way to their dreams, whether it's boosting your rates, transitioning to speaking and consulting, creating a legacy for family or the world, simply becoming a "published author," or becoming a full-time author.

It's no longer a matter of gaining the approval of a publisher or of "who you know." It's now a *science,* achievable by anyone with a bit of intelligence, perseverance, and passion. In fact, there's a formula for author success:

$$List \ x \ List = Viability$$

Where one list is your *email list of readers,* and the other your *backlist of related of books.* "Viability" in this formula is money, basically.

But even with *one book* I've seen so many lives changed, so many dreams come true:

- One person in Fort Lauderdale wrote a book about the crazy days of spring break in the 70s and now, decades later, walks bar-to-bar selling hard copies for $20, eking out a living sans a "job."

- A computer programmer lands a $10,000 project because someone found his website, ordered and read his book that same night, and hired him without batting an eye the next morning a 9 a.m.

- Dr. Joseph Rosado, M.D.[10], the pioneer in the field of medical cannabis in Florida, releases his first book, *Hope & Healing,* and now tours the *world,* consulting both professionals and governments.

And so many more great examples of doing it right, not the least of which include the biographies, the lessons in narcissism, that children's book, *your book on an end cap in Barnes & Noble,* and so much more. And what if your great-

---

[10] https://www.josephrosadomd.com/

grandfather or great-grandmother wrote a memoir, how cool would that be to read?

We all define "success" a bit differently, but we all also have abundant proof that *books change lives.*

Science, not luck.

In any trade or profession, there are a limited number of terms that make you conversant in that subject and start you on the road to certainty and success. In publishing, the terms have changed, *a lot* in some cases, and author-clients are, frankly, being taken advantage of, particularly by "best seller mills" calling themselves "publishers" but who have no interest in more than your cash. It started perhaps as "vanity publishing," a term not heard much anymore, but the modern, competent, certain, self-published author understands the changes in meaning some terms have undergone.

I've found defining things like "publisher" and "best seller" protects modern authors and helps them plan, and throughout this book we'll clear up all the useful and important ones I can think of.

THE MODERN AUTHOR

The modern author knows the current publishing industry. They know the Book Creation Cycle. They produce the best possible book(s) and are savvy and confident on launch day and beyond. They know their publishing and distribution options and cater their plan to their own goals.

The modern author sees it all from 30,000 feet. The modern author does it all by their lonesome if they choose, or they hire a collaborator or consultant, assemble a team of independent contractors, buy a package from a hybrid publishing house, crowdfund their way to a good match in a publisher with Publishizer.com, or land a traditional publishing deal.

But whatever they choose, the modern author is aware of and has myriad choices.

MODERN MEANINGS:

LEARNING, IGNORANCE
& WORDS

"My lips are moving and the sound's coming out
The words are audible but I have my doubts
That you realize what has been said
You look at me as if you're in a daze
It's like the feeling at the end of the page
When you realize you don't know what you just read"

—From the song, "Words," by the band
MISSING PERSONS

HOW IMPORTANT are the meanings of words? How about *very*. Maybe more than very. I'm sure you can think of plenty of examples, maybe funny ones, but a wrong or altered (or lack of any) meaning can have disastrous or at least embarrassing or frustrating consequences. Never more true than in publishing today.

How important is *learning?* Put it this way, one of our librarians here just told me a patron has various games and puzzles around her house because she swears having these constant challenges *produces* grey matter, and evidently keeps her vibrant and growing *at 97.* I've heard we make new neural connections with learning *new* things, but I guess I'd not heard we create additional "grey matter." For this and so many reasons, I (and Thomas Jefferson and others) highly value *self-education.* My gut tells me this little bit on learning is important because as I started in self-publishing I learned a lot quickly by *copying*—the layout of books, cover designs, writing styles. So maybe a thought or two on *learning* can speed up your own path to becoming a modern author.

LEARNING

"Writing is learned by imitation.
If anyone asked me how I learned to write,
I'd say I learned by reading the men and
women who were doing the kind of writing
I wanted to do and trying to figure out how
they did it."

— WILLIAM ZINSSER

I learned book design first simply by modeling, and then by *The Chicago Manual of Style,* which I was introduced to by a snotty editor who, when many years ago I expressed an interest in being an editor myself, snooted, "Oh really? Which methodology do you use?" In pursuit of the best answer for me and the kinds of books I was working on, I found *CMOS.* I then found two websites that laid out customary *parts of a book.* (We list them all in *Book 2: The Book Creation Cycle.*)

Then as now, I am (we are all) faced with *learning* as one of the most fundamental and enjoyable aspects of the game of life, certainly any career.

When I was 40 and went back to the University of Florida, I was deeply grateful for the courses, this time around. And I was introduced to the idea of *pedagogy*[11], or methods of teaching and learning. And when homeschooling my daughter, I found we learn according to *personal learning styles*. Here are a few I really like—because if you're aware of these, you can more easily learn anything:

- **Modeling**, which is to say, *copying* but including your own transformations

- **Analogy**, as things compared to other things leads to clarity

- **Study**

- **Observation**

- **Experience**

- **Extremes**, if you take something to extremes, it can be revealing. I had a friend who told another friend he'd found a job selling boas[12] at strip clubs. I asked, "Does he plan to make a career of that?" And we

---

[11] pedagogy, noun: the art, science, or profession of teaching — https://www.merriam-webster.com/dictionary/pedagogy

[12] A boa is a fashion accessory that is usually worn wrapped around the neck like a scarf. Feather boas are most common, although modern boas are most often made with synthetic feathers. —Wikipedia

laughed, picturing him pimped-out, when we both knew Chris. It made me see how running something to an extreme can inform if I should bother with it at all, looking at futures with it, extrapolating.

- Of course, the first barrier to learning is *interest,* expressed by *asking*.

I think it's *really* important to add, even while this is not a "treatise on pedagogy" and only included because as indies we are all about to start and continue learning—in fact it's a major facet of joy in life—that learning is *not only inflow, and that inflow alone is indoctrination.* Blecch. Exploring your interests, asking questions, going out and looking, reading books, objective thinking, discussion and debate, even nice walks, all add to enrichment. As indies we get to choose, more and more, what we spend our precious time and energy wondering, thinking about, concluding—and here's where the indie part comes in—sharing.

Most of all, I say let your interest lead you, as much as you have the luxury. Learning is supposed to be part of the joy of living.

> "The best way to kill a love
> is to turn it into a labor."
>
> — PAUL CHEK, Educator

WORDS

The following updated definitions might save you a lot of time, heartache, embarrassment, and cash, and are shared here to give you clarity and a chance at professionalism in your publishing. Note that things change. In fact, I now have a thirteen-plus-year career and experience to reflect upon. In that time "self-publishing" (as a term) has gone from taboo to something to be proud of. There are many examples of significant and important changes *in meaning*, so stay flexible as you move forward. Situational awareness! All of these affect publishing, whether you're in it for your memoir, book of expertise, and especially if you are envisioning a career (or retirement) as an author.

"IGNORANCE GAP"

This is what I call the difference between what's in your mind and what's in reality, if different. Certain terms have evolved over the years since the introduction of digital publishing, print-on-demand publishing, and self-publishing in general (although people have on occasion "self-published" throughout history, however difficult). So if someone suggests they can make you a "best-selling author" (for a fee), make sure they mean what you think they mean! It might not be they can get you on the *New York Times* Best Seller List with thousands of sales during a big hoopla of a launch week; it might be they know how to place you in an Amazon *niche category* with little competition where you can be ranked in the top 100 books *and almost no sales*. Both scenarios are technically "best sellers," as we'll discuss.

If you are aware of these *ignorance gaps* you can simply avoid or step over them, or get terms better defined, and make actual plans that achieve your hopes and dreams for your book and author career, if that's what you seek. And that's one of the major importances *of the book you hold,* it eliminates *ignorance gaps.*

"Best Seller"

(Commonly spelled either "best seller" or "bestseller.") Ever hear "caveat emptor[13]?" People still generally believe that a "best seller" has sold lots and lots of copies, but that's not always the case.

Did you know you can create a "best seller" in a few days sometimes without selling a single copy of your book?

The confusion is often used by the unscrupulous to take advantage of uninformed authors (which you are really not, not any longer) and exploit the ignorance gap. In the past, and still the most prominent, the *New York Times* Best Seller List came out weekly and included about 25 titles that met "their criteria." Years ago, this typically included hardcover titles. This alone might explain the apparent traditional publisher approach to release a hardcover edition and let it sell for a year before releasing a paperback (and later on an ebook and

---

[13] *Caveat emptor* is a common law doctrine that places the burden on buyers to reasonably examine property before making a purchase. A buyer who fails to meet this burden is unable to recover for defects in the product that would have been discovered had this burden been met. The phrase "caveat emptor" is Latin for "let the buyer beware."
—https://www.law.cornell.edu/wex/caveat_emptor

audiobook edition). Sales (just one criterion) were measured in one-week periods, running Monday through Sunday, and reported by bookstores to a company/service called BookScan, which was (not any longer) owned by Nielsen (ratings/market research).

People then and now assume if your book appears on the *New York Times* Best Seller List it is perhaps one of 25 or so *top books in the world.* And many simply buy their next read from such best seller lists, so the topic is important to us.

Well, between then and now, a lot has changed. For one, the *New York Times* admitted before the Supreme Court of all places, that their rankings are not strictly based on sales. (Go ahead, read that again.) In fact, in an excellent article by Tucker Max on the subject of best sellers (link in the footnotes):

> "Make no mistake about it --
> this is all just as elitist and snobbish as it
> sounds. They (*New York Times*) only
> recently started including ebooks in their
> lists, and they still heavily discount ebooks
> that have no print edition. Yes they track
> them, but they count their sales as less…
> The reality is that even though the *New
> York Times* list is seen as the most
> prestigious, in many ways it's the least
> connected to actual book selling reality.[14]"

If we back up a second, many still have the prestigious version of *best seller* in their minds, even as an ultimate goal

---

[14] https://www.entrepreneur.com/leadership/how-best seller-lists-actually-work-and-how-to-get-on-them/280520

for writing and publishing a book! And that's all good. What I want you to recognize are the sharks who promise to make your book a "best seller" as part of an upfront fee or paid program. Let me explain why.

Enter Amazon, and this is another big change in this subject (best sellers) in the last 20 years. Instead of a couple of lists each with about 25 titles from a few dozen genres, Amazon introduced *hundreds* of their own categories, each with its own Top 100 books noted as best sellers, as well as other best seller lists, such as an overall Top 100 list. And rather than the rankings changing every week, Amazon updates these rankings *every hour.*

In fact Amazon's approach to best sellers has evolved, but when someone is using the ignorance gap to appeal to your ego or at least your worthy goal to get on "the" best seller list, when they promise to make you a "best seller" (for a fee) you need to know the dirty little secret in publishing: It was possible (not as much now) to place your book in a niche category with less than 100 titles and your book would be considered a "best seller" by Amazon in that category, *even if it never sold a single book.* It even appears *as a best seller on the chart for that category on Amazon.* It was simply based on the top 100 books in any category, and there used to be categories with fewer than 100 books!

I always explain this when it's a stated author-client goal (there are different strategies for the different lists which I explain as well), and many clients don't care, they want this status as a credibility point. All good! And yes, it looks and sounds great. My belief is the public, as their purchases lead them to more discernment, will start to differentiate between the different lists, because so many books and authors now claim to be "best sellers," something gives! Still good, though. But I wince a little when a book or author claims to be a best seller and their book isn't even what I call "healthy," or for example, has less than 15 reviews on Amazon. "Best seller?"

You just don't want your marketing effort and investment to *backfire.* And there are, in my opinion, *more reasons to skip focus on best seller lists than to strive for them.* Counter-intuitive, right?

So why would one *not* want to strive for these lists?

- It puts attention, energy, and resources on a sort of false goal, if it's simply a feeding of your ego. Those resources might have been better spent on things that actually accomplish your *true goals,* which are what I always discuss with clients at the outset of any project.

- It's often a subjective thing you cannot guarantee, and can set you up for failure.

And why would one *want* to make a best seller list, and maybe make that a priority in launching? ("When" doesn't matter, you can get on a best seller list at any time.)

- Best seller lists sell books! But what it takes to get on them should be considered, along with whatever opportunity cost they involve.

- You might be building a personal brand and being a "best-selling author" is an important part of that.

- It might be a lifelong dream of yours!

If that's the case, great! You should still know the above and that there are now many options and *types* of best seller lists, and all of this is subject to change, *and it does.*

A few more thoughts on "best sellers:"

- It apparently takes anywhere from 3,000 to 10,000 sales in any given week to be considered for the *New York Times* list, and that a sort of prom committee chooses books for the list, based partly on sales and on other, often subjective, criteria. I've also read that "elite" publishing houses often make a call to the *New York Times* to alert them to certain books, which then get attention, something an indie can't really do.

- The *USA Today* list is one that seems more scientific in that they go more by actual sales numbers without the prejudices of the *New York Times,* and many indie authors have made this list apparently with as few as 3,000 sales in a week, selling their books on a variety of platforms (a seeming requirement).

- The *Wall Street Journal* list seems to follow *USA Today,* so indies who make *USA Today* seem to also make *WSJ.*

- **Amazon** now has several types of lists—smaller ones for each and every category, and their "Top 100" which takes a lot more sales than the niche-category lists. Amazon lists are the most commonly strived for in the indie community.

In any case, seeking best seller status usually requires you concentrate your sales through a certain channel or channels during a certain period of time (a day or a week). If you look at the different best seller lists each week, you'll notice they are not all the same. That alone tells you they have different criteria. People have sought ways to game the systems and even to buy their way on to particular lists with as much as $150,000 to buy onto the *NYT* list—not as a direct bribe (lol) but to someone who games the system by using part of that moolah to buy your book in bulk, if bulk sales are still counted by *NYT* when you're reading this. They used to be, marked to reflect the fact, but still counted. The point is there is reason for these platforms to keep their criteria and procedures confidential, and to change them when warranted.

Whatever you decide, all good, but know this: When the tide goes out, you see who has been swimming naked. The "public" adapt. Mark my words, it may not be the case now, but there will come a day when you say to someone, "Well, I'm a best-selling author."

And they say, "Really? What kind?"

I mean, we compare types of milk and other things, right?

Choosing to make a best seller list part of your priorities is fine—it's great, actually—as long as you're aware of the above. How this affects your launch and planning will be discussed in those sections, no worries.

"LITERACY"

Literacy means you can read, right? Yes, it does. It's worth noting, though, that if we went from an illiterate state to a literate one, *that transition would have been a kind of miracle,* tantamount to perhaps suddenly being able to communicate telepathically. Think about that group of cavepeople when that first one said, "Grrr, ugh, no go that way!" followed by the word for "bear." What did that little expression of thought save that tribe? How much time did it save that caveman who no longer had to act out "bear," and that *there was one, right over there?*

Literacy—fast, certain, efficient, important.

And what does *illiteracy* mean? I took it for granted until as a young man I met an old man in a grocery store who asked me to read a label for him. He didn't seem to lack vision, and I remember my heart sank. *He can't seem to read.*

Literacy is a gift we enjoy and often take for granted. It can always be improved and it can be taught. It plays a role in thinking about who your audience will be for your book. In the main, over these last 13 years I have collaborated with authors who wrote for a "popular audience," meaning your average Joe (books of expertise, memoirs, fiction for us common people, as opposed to white papers, academic reports, etc.). So, write, speak, edit, communicate accordingly.

In fact, when preparing and reviewing your own book, I recommend we follow a path of escalation of exposure:

1. You alone

2. You and I (as we create your content, back and forth)

3. Once we're "getting there" *you now review* not as the writer but through the *eyes of a reader*

4. You and I and your *alpha reader* (simply, the first "other" you share with, often a spouse or friend) once we're "almost/maybe there"

5. You and I, your alpha, and a short list of *beta readers* once your draft is "ready for reviewers"

6. The World

This is a good path for gradual "coming out" of your book and the above process if followed results in an author who is *confident, ready,* and ideally *excited* about the release of their book. And it works, I've done it with *this book.*

But on the larger subject of *reading,* thirteen years ago at the age of 40, I went back to college and rather than change the definition of literacy, a wonderful professor at the University of Florida coined a new term for the modern age…

"ELECTRACY"

Coined by Professor Gregory Ulmer, *electracy* "is to digital media what literacy is to print[15]." It "describes the kind of 'literacy' or skill and facility necessary to exploit the full communicative potential of new electronic media such as multimedia, hypermedia, social software, and virtual worlds.[16]"

---

[15] Ulmer, G. L. (2003). *Internet Invention: From Literacy to Electracy.* New York: Longman.
[16] http://www.rhizomes.net/issue18/ulmer/index.html, accessed October 16, 2022

"It encompasses the broader cultural, institutional, pedagogical, and ideological implications inherent in the major societal transition from print to electronic media.[17]"

But more than that, "a basic feature of electracy: that communicating at light-speed is done by means of emblems, slogans, mottos, logos (whether Aristotle's *logos* to corporate logos).[18]"

Put more simply, it's what kids seem to do naturally. I remember my little daughter showing my stepfather how to work a DVD player, for example. But even more—and this is one reason I include the term—the idea that an emblem or logo or image or color communicates almost instantly, and often communicates meaning, memory, emotion, and sets expectations. This will be very important when we design book covers, for one thing (and in any branding and marketing you do).

If we are to believe the common narrative, civilization has gone from illiterate grunting, to cave paintings, to re-enactments, to "stories" acted out in songs and ceremonies that relay history and other information *without* writing, to writing, to the printing press for mass inclusion and dispersal of knowledge, to the electronic forms of relay of information we all now enjoy. Our ability to assimilate this information is now called *electracy,* a step beyond *literacy.*

As I write this, AI is fast becoming a new factor in how we seek information and the speed and quantity with which it is delivered. I shudder a bit, as so many fools in their excitement are likely to surrender too much control to AI, as it's thus far *intelligence without conscience*, or as American General Douglas Macgregor recently said, "AI is just a better

---

[17] https://en.wikipedia.org/wiki/Electracy, accessed October 16, 2022

[18] http://www.rhizomes.net/issue18/ulmer/index.html, accessed October 16, 2022

algorithm." But it all remains to be seen, of course. Meanwhile, things like ChatGPT can take research and writing to speeds not before imagined, even with the internet.

"WRITER"

On a wonderful episode of *The Best Seller Experiment* podcast[19], a caller kind of apologized, "Well, I'm not really a writer yet."

Their guest, author Joanne Harris[20] asked, "Well, do you write?"

"Yes, I guess so. I'm aspiring to be a writer."

"Take the aspiring out of it," she said. "If you write, then you are a writer."

We'll expand a little when we define "writing" a few pages from now, but in the trade (ghostwriting, writing, editing, publishing, etc.) we refer to clients as "authors" and their writers as "writers." (I refer to my clients as "author-clients.") Because *if you write, you are a writer, no matter the means of writing. And if you publish or are publishing a book, you are an author.*

"AUTHOR"

So, a writer writes, but an *author* writes a *book* or books and ideally, is published. "Author" can of course be used in other ways, such as "author of the Bill of Rights," but for our

---

[19] https://best sellerexperiment.com/
[20] http://www.joanne-harris.co.uk/

purposes an author writes a book, or is the source of thought and direction in a book project where a writer assists.

Part of the differentiation for me came through the years when I was asked what I do. I thought about it, and as I had been a ghostwriter, then a "book collaborator," I felt comfortable saying, "I'm a writer." (That felt great to say, too.) I realized that if I had said, "I'm an author," the expectation—mine, anyway—would be that I make the majority of my income from royalties from books I've written and published. And I had not achieved that yet. The clients I assist and coach who are methodically building author careers even as they work a day job, certainly deserve to be called "authors." Because they are.

"BOOK"

Here's where the remainder of these definitions might get really interesting. The digital age has changed so much. Once upon a time a "book" was meticulously written by hand, bound, and sold or shared among those fortunate enough to be literate and able to afford a *book*. Mass production didn't change the basic premise of a book—a cover and pages bound with something to read and/or see inside.

Today a "book" might be a digital file on an e-reader like a Nook or Kindle, or on your phone or tablet. It might also be a recording *of a book* you listen to. Still a book—an *audio*book.

Expect new forms to appear in the future. In fact in science fiction, an adage is that *the further into the future you write, the more the technology will seem like magic.*

"READING"

Reading traditionally means looking with your eyes at packages of thought (words) strung together into larger concepts and descriptions of action and ideas which themselves string together into larger ideas and virtual experiences, with the purposes of entertainment and education. This is understood to take place with the aid of a traditional "book," being ink-on-paper pages bound between the front and back and spine of protective covering.

But what about a blind person reading in braille? What if you're jogging on a treadmill or driving in a car, listening to an audiobook? Still "reading" if you ask me. And if Neo plugs a rod into the back of his head and learns Kung Fu at the speed of the download, not only is that "reading," it's a proof of Professor Ulmer's definition of *electracy,* that what is transmitted by digital means is assimilated (and how well determines how *electrate* you might be). So, *reading is the assimilation of information.* That understanding is right there in our language when we say things like "I found him hard to read," for example. Assimilation by various means, but it's also implied that there's an *understanding.* And so, *reading is assimilation with understanding regardless of means.*

One thing I took from James Patterson is the idea that reading gives us a sense of accomplishment. I used to feel sort of obligated to read or complete a read. I think it came from being forced to read in school. In fact, I found myself later in life choosing a book and trudging through even if it hadn't captured me, making note of page numbers and progress as I went, even setting little goals like, "Read at least 50 pages a day," but it didn't work. What has worked is having an *abundance* mindset when it comes to reading, which means being willing to waste a book here and there. If a book doesn't catch me pretty quickly or if I find myself keeping track of page numbers or losing track too often, I put it down, with few exceptions.

One added note I found interesting, for whatever it's worth. While waiting with my mother at her eye surgeon's office, a screen came on the TV that stated, "People tend to read 25 percent slower on screen than on paper." Interesting! I get headaches from too much screen time. And I prefer paperback, or hardcover, and hardly ever read eBooks. Maybe that's because I'm 53 or maybe it's because I spend so much time with a computer screen as it is, I don't know. Maybe I like the look and feel of *a print book.* Regardless, interesting, right? More on this in Book 2 (or maybe Book 3, remains to be seen) where we'll talk a lot about author productivity.

Either way, please consider…

It's okay to put a book down.

For this reason I usually test drive a book from the library before buying it. (Also because by now we've pared down so many times, adopting a lightweight, travel-friendly lifestyle without a lot of crap to move around). Or I buy the cheaper ebook and once I know I like it buy a print edition. There are titles I set aside and read later, but *read what you like,* for Pete's sake.

*Today, there are over one million books
published each year.*

So, you have *lots* of choices. If one author on a subject doesn't appeal to you, another likely will. Keep looking, and enjoy! Of course, *I love to read what I love to read.* Additionally, some books are better than others. In fact I've categorized books (for a practical purpose for self-publishers), and this categorization plays an important role in your planning as a self-published, modern author:

- Books that suck

- Good books

- Great books

- Healthy books

- Seasoned books

- Successful books

- Phenomenal books

I submit that a book of *any genre* can be catalogued according to the above, fitting into one or several of those categories. This makes it more clear what you might want to achieve with your book. And if you embrace reading, which usually means *making time* on a couch or in bed or in the bathroom to simply *read,* the joy can be reignited, or maybe discovered for the first time. *Reading is for you.* And the world unfolds for us who read. Just don't brag about how much or what you've read. I just ate a salad, but you don't see me bragging about it.

I wanted to touch on *reading* because, as so many writers will tell you, it is likely the most neglected aspect of *writing*. Reading is an inflow, and writing is an outflow, and it might be that we are at our best when the two are in balance.

Put a small bookshelf in the bathroom, if that's what it takes. It's supposed to be enlightening, or fun escapism, or stimulate learning. Enjoy it, make time for it, make sure it flows. Don't think of it as work.

"The beginning of wisdom
is the definition of terms."

— SOCRATES

PART I

MODERN

PUBLISHING

———————

"It's never been easier to share your
ideas and passions with the world."

— PETER DIAMANDIS

THE DAWN OF DIGITAL
PUBLISHING

A BRIEF HISTORY of self-publishing, even if from my
modest perspective, might explain who the players are
today, a bit about how and why modern self-
publishing platforms behave, and what it means to be a
modern author. In fact, it should help you understand your

publishing options today (they're great), and enable you to design your own best path for success with your book(s).

A few years before I was in the business, the first self-published book I ever read was written, designed, and self-published by a friend of mine. It had a lot of good, useful information, actually, which made it well worth the price despite its flaws, and it impressed me that my friend knew what he did about the subject (and that he self-published a book, long before I ever did). The cover looked pretty good but I could tell Alan had designed it himself. When I read the book I was alarmed because it seemed like no editing had taken place, at all. It became a distraction and made me concerned others would miss his message somewhere in the poor grammar and lack of editing, when *what he must have been seeking for himself was some form of success with his book.*

He wrote a great book! But the lack of editing and lack of professional design left doubt, as it was a "book of expertise." And unpolished *production* can make your book of expertise *backfire.*

This was the initial problem with self-publishing, that the gatekeepers were no longer keeping gates, there was no publisher involved in a self-published book to ensure it had good content or was presented professionally, at least not until the standards kind of found a waterline in the industry.

Since then I've learned, and I've designed what I call the *Book Creation Cycle.* I've learned it in my time creating books by seeking out best practices. I learned from reading and study of the business, from experience with it, and from people I've worked with in both traditional and self-publishing. Today, you have so many options as an "indie," your results can be as or even more professional than the big publishing houses.

As more indies learn and implement best practices of self-publishing, the whole industry rises in the public's eyes, as well as with booksellers, and that will keep creating new opportunities for us all. For example, I just walked into the Orlando Airport with four sample books and four *book one sheets* and luckily met a regional manager of a chain with 360 stores that sell books. He took the samples and seemed wide open to considering them, never asking who my publisher was. I truly believe any interest they will or won't have will be based on the potential fit the books might have in their stores, and of course, the quality of the books.

WHY PUBLISH
TRADITIONALLY

So, why do we still have "traditional publishers?" And why would anyone consider them? What I believe traditional (New York, especially) publishers are good at includes:

1. *New York Times* **Best Seller List** achievement, if this is a dream of yours.

2. **Full-service distribution**, meaning they will push your book onto the shelves in bookstores (traditionally-published authors make more of their income from print, where indies make more from ebooks), although you can do this for yourself if you set your book up correctly with IngramSpark and do the work to get your book placed on shelves in bookstores.

3. **Competitive hardcover pricing,** as they print in large *offset print runs[21],* whereas indies can create hardcover editions but suffer higher production costs as we typically opt for print-on-demand.

4. **Access to professional in-house editing and design,** although you can choose your own editor and designers with ease by referral, with freelance platforms like Upwork, Reedsy, or with consultants and other service providers (like me) or small self-publishing assistance companies, or you can find a mastermind or book like this one and DIY.

5. Established access to and influence with **national media.**

WHY NOT PUBLISH TRADITIONALLY

As you might see, most of this you can do on your own, without waiting years for a publisher to pick you up and invest their $ in your project, without contracts full of legalese, without sacrificing a share of the creativity, without giving up 15 to 85 percent of your royalties, and without giving up rights to your book. Most traditional publishers will want a contract and to own your ISBNs and to own your web domain to keep you "committed."

---

[21] Offset printing is a commercial printing process used for large print runs of books, business cards, magazines, and posters. — https://www.chilliprinting.com/Online-Printing-Blog/print-on-demand-vs-offset-printing/

Traditional publishers still have a valuable role to play (although I know I don't make it sound that way).

You should also know they often keep a loss leader for the prestige and to keep the little guys eager to be a part. Your top, household author names are said to *cost* a publisher money rather than make it for them on occasion, but are kept as window dressing and for credibility. The moolah might be easier had on smaller writers like us. Wouldn't it be appealing, after all, to be in the same stable as Stephen King, Danielle Steel, or Dr. Suess?[22]

From my view, pitfalls of traditional publishing include:

1. **Finding one!** It typically takes a finished book or long-form book proposal (depending on your genre) presented along with a query letter *and luck* to make it through the first gate, a literary agent. Many publishers won't even consider a book not presented by an agent who shops your book to publishing houses. Then, finding a traditional publisher who believes in and knows how to sell your book can take years or never happen at all. In today's world, it has been said, "The ebook is the new query letter," meaning your successful self-published book will be what gets the interest of a traditional publisher. And perhaps much more quickly.

2. They take a large **percent of your profits**. I listened to an interesting interview on the radio one night where a rock band explained they self-published their album because to make a profit with the record label they needed to sell tens of thousands of copies, versus a few thousand on their own, and they had

---

[22] https://en.wikipedia.org/wiki/List_of_best-selling_fiction_authors

the skills needed, anyway. *In fact, in this digital age, we have many of the skills needed already.* And they did succeed on their own as they expected, evidenced by being on the radio, where I found them.

3. They often exert **unwanted creative influence or control** over your book, sometimes warranted, sometimes strictly business.

4. They usually **share in your rights**, so when you are approached about a movie deal or animation rights, for example, or even something seemingly obscure like "digital rights in the U.K," they have a stake and a say, and a share. (If this happily happens and you are self-published, there are many professionals who can look over your offer and advise you for a fee and without self-interest.)

5. They can become a **bottleneck or even an outright barrier** to changing your price, book description, keywords, access to sales data, and more. They might own your ISBNs and web domain as well.

6. Often a surprise to the author, *you* are expected to **do your own marketing** and **pay your own marketing costs**, which is hard to swallow when giving up 50 to 85 percent of your royalties.

7. But the very worst case is where your book does not pay out at launch and they **simply drop their interest** in you, despite the remaining years under contract.

All that said, 100 percent of zero is... zero. So if a traditional publisher really believes in your book, even 5 percent of a million is... well you do the math.

The point is traditional publishing is now not the only path, it's simply one of the many options available today to the modern author, and not even the best option in so many cases.

It's horrible but with one exception, those authors I personally know who have been lucky enough to get a traditional publishing deal then spent months trying to get out of those deals.

An author-client from New York City knew an old-time publisher who she told about the book we were working on to see if he had any interest. He was brutally honest:

"Will it sell?" he asked. "Why should I get involved?"

And the takeaway from this is actually a helpful thing to understand, a positive, even. Publishing is a business, and publishers usually have a niche they are familiar with. I have tried in the past to explain to discouraged authors who have been turned down by traditional publishers, "It may have nothing to do with the quality or merit of your book. It has everything to do with that publisher knowing how to sell your book." And the smart ones usually know what they know, and avoid new genres or learning curves.

Traditional publishing, formerly the only way to sell books, is now an *option.* And for some of us, you might want a traditional publisher *if* they have valuable expertise and connections to national media, cost-effective connections for print runs (especially hardback), and *full-service distribution* to bookstores. *There are great reasons to be traditionally published.* I got to work a little once for a longtime, successful, traditionally-published author and she never planned to leave traditional publishing. She was self-publishing a side project book outside her regular genre and remarked on how hands-on self-publishing was, and how she really liked the ability to focus on writing while her publisher took care of the myriad things indies do for themselves. When she explained, it sounded like a breath of fresh air.

PUBLISHING TODAY

Thanks to the creative disruption in publishing caused by the Internet, Amazon, and other factors, it's not just authors who have seen a metamorphosis. Publishing itself has been utterly transformed. But if you ask me, it seems the same functions still exist. In other words, when you learn the Book Creation Cycle, *those ten steps that lead to optimized books* are what better traditional publishers do anyway, if slightly modified for self-publishing. Again, you can do most or all of those ten steps all yourself, or with an editor, or assemble a team for it, or hand it over to a "publisher" or "consultant" who will guide you through each stage.

THE BOOK CREATION CYCLE

I have for over a decade now called myself a "collaborator," as I did not want anyone to confuse what I do with traditional publishing. I also no longer wanted to be a "ghostwriter" because I wanted to start earning name credits and building a portfolio I could share. "Self-publishing consultant" fits, but I don't just consult, I perform "author services" and I guide and help authors with all ten stages of the Book Creation Cycle, which are:

1. Planning

2. Writing

3. Editing

4. Design

5. Marketing

6. Production

7. Distribution

8. Pre-launch

9. Launch

10. Post-launch

Note that if you "write to market," marketing is second, rather than fifth, and also note this is the procedure of *best practices* for creating a professionally-done book, and does not include author platform growth (well, maybe a little) and many other things important to self-published authors ("indies").

CONTRACTORS, TEAMS, & COMPANIES

I've already stated my opinion of those "publishers" who exploit your perhaps grander idea of publishing for their upfront fees, but that does not mean every publisher who charges up-front fees is a sham. In fact such are simply called "service publishers," which is what I might be, except that I stamp your own publishing imprint on your book, not mine. And I don't pay advances or share in your rights or royalties. (But I have realized now that I manage platform development and other tasks for a short list of authors on an ongoing basis, I'm becoming more of a "for-hire publisher.")

Today "publisher" does not just mean a handful of executives in a tower in Manhattan. Today there is a *gradient scale* of publishing service providers, aka "publishers." You are about to read up on those types of publishers, and it will all start to make sense. You'll be informed and prepared to make decisions that best suit *you*, another milestone in becoming a modern author.

You can go it alone, you can form a team (small or large), and/or you can hire a company or find a reputable publisher such as BookBaby, Morgan James, and others. I have limited experience with them but as far as I know they have been around as long as I have—a very good sign.

Me, I'm an advocate of working with *individuals* because you form a personal relationship, there's more accountability, and there's less bureaucracy, less passing you around. I'm for piecing together your team as you see fit, whether it's one dude or a handful of people. I've worked and collaborated in many such arrangements. In many cases I do my part and basically hand the project off to the next team member, freelancer, or company, such as the author-client's web designer, existing marketing person, or company.

By the way, marketing *books* is unique. I've worked with very savvy, established, even well-known marketers, some who can and some who can't sell books. Maybe they can create goodwill, do public relations, get their clients on podcasts, interviews, and stage, design effective SEO, write effective copy, and implement and manage ad campaigns much better than I can, but many just don't seem to know how to *sell books.* It's not an insult, either, it's a specialty. Often we simply work as a team because while they write great copy, create funnels, and manage ad campaigns, I often know *where* they should place the ads, for example. I often hang around as a consultant in such situations, even after the book is live.

As you seek out team members for your book project, find out what they are great at, allow some overlap with the other pros you add to the team, clearly define roles, and go for it. Such professionals might include:

- Marketers

- Publicity

- Web design

- Branding

- SEO experts

- Content and social media marketing

Or find a firm that does books. Smith Publicity, for example, has focused on books as a PR firm for decades. They have (or had) a relatively affordable flat-fee program that guaranteed you got on something like 30 podcast interviews. Forbes has author launch services, I just found out thanks to a client, and they endorse another firm (Advantage Media) for books and authors who are already published, helping with national media, and we're looking into this at this writing. Or, one client and I went over a number of professionals' *own social media followings* to see if they do for themselves what they offer to do for you, and with surprising (often disappointing) results.

I try to actually meet and talk with professionals in adjacent fields so when I find good ones I can have ready suggestions when author-clients ask or I think they'd fit the project. Often it's author-clients who bring them to my attention. They might be great not only for your book, but your business or cause.

TYPES OF MODERN PUBLISHERS[23]

But back to *types of modern publishers*. Today, we can break them down into three basic categories:

---

[23] Grateful acknowledgement to the bright minds at Publishizer, who described so well the new forms of publishers today and innovated a short form of book proposal. Although their focus is matching you with a *traditional publisher,* these ideas are powerful for indies, both in understanding modern publishing and in starting off your marketing. Check them out at https://publishizer.com/.

1. Those who charge up-front fees ("service" or "hybrid" publishers)

2. Those who charge back-end fees (usually buying a minimum quantity of copies through them)

3. Those who make money by sharing royalties and might even pay advances (more traditional publishers)

Publishizer expands this list into *five* types of modern publishers:

1. **Big Five**[24]—When I started thirteen years ago it was the Big Six, now the Big Five:

   1) Penguin Random House

   2) Simon & Schuster

   3) Hachette

   4) HarperCollins

   5) Macmillan

---

[24] Excellent article on larger publishers and their histories (in brief) can be found here: https://www.book-editing.com/the-big-5-trade-publishers-and-their-imprints/

2. Traditional publishers

3. Independent publishers

4. Hybrid publishers

5. Service publishers, which is what I would be. Although I *am* a publisher, I either guide and consult indies as "work for hire[25]" (service publisher), or have my own small publishing "imprints[26]" such as Powers Press for my *Inspiring Women Today* series or Rodney Miles for other titles.

And here's how they are different, generally[27]:

1. Big Five publishers:

   o Do not charge costs

   o Pay highest advances

   o Royalties: Expect 5-15%

   o Perks: Prestige, publicity

---

[25] "Work for hire" implies the person hiring the writing, for example, owns the copyright (and they do as long as their invoices are paid!).

[26] An imprint of a publisher is a trade name under which it publishes a work. A single publishing company may have multiple imprints, often using the different names as brands to market works to various demographic consumer segments. — Wikipedia

[27] https://publishizer.com/

2. Traditional publishers:

  o   Do not charge costs

  o   Pay high advances

  o   Royalties: Expect 10-20%

  o   Perks: Distribution, credibility

3. Independent publishers:

  o   Do not charge costs

  o   Pay modest advances

  o   Royalties: Expect 15-50%

  o   Perks: Credibility, service

4. Hybrid publishers:

  o   May charge costs

  o   Do not pay advances

  o   Royalties: Expect 50-100%

  o   Perks: Flexibility, speed

5. Service publishers:

    o   Do charge costs

    o   Do not pay advances

    o   Royalties: 100%

    o   Perks: Control, ownership

Again, credit to Lee Constantine and Publishizer.com. They've contributed to modern publishing just by describing these things, and their short-form book proposal is *brilliant.* It's a staple in my marketing recommendations early on. And if you are interested in seeing how you do with a campaign there and what publishers they match you up with, *do it!* The process of running a Publishizer campaign is enlightening and your results, large or small, naturally guide you to a likely fit for where you are in your author career. It's a way to find a traditional deal or to be matched with service providers.

Understanding the modern forms of publisher today will make life and publishing easier as an author. It will also *protect you* from those who are unclear or tricky in their marketing. You might even become a publisher, yourself! I've had several clients not only continue to write and publish books once they knew how, but who took the imprint we came up with and start their own companies.

Remember, with the know-how of the Book Creation Cycle, you can do it all or pick and choose what parts you might like to do and hire the rest. It all depends on your goals, talents, time, budget, and other resources, of course.

SO, SHOULD I
SELF-PUBLISH?

Yes, especially your first book. And in most cases, every book after that. Remember, when you retain most or all of your rights and royalties, retain your creative freedom, and are the master of your own business decisions and actions, you are *self-published*, even if you had help, at least in my book. (See what I did there?)

And as far as *at least* self-publishing your first book, I fall back on Carlton Sheets, remember him? When I was a kid he was known for late-night TV commercials for his course, *No Down Payment*. He advocated managing your first rental properties by yourself because you learn the process and learn also how to manage your soon-to-be-hired property manager.

Makes a lot of sense, but there is one caveat: If your dream is still a traditional publishing deal, most traditional publishers I have any experience with will only take on your book *before* it is published. You can re-launch a book, and it can become a best seller at any time, but they all seem to feel they'd rather work with you on your *next* book than on one that is already available, regardless. I say this because at least two or three prospective author-clients (in 13 years) have *insisted* on finding a traditional publisher. For that, they don't need me, they need either a finished manuscript or a full book proposal and, usually, a literary agent.

WHAT STINKS ABOUT SELF-PUBLISHING?

Think of it like cooking. If you go traditional let's say that's like dining out all the time. And let's compare self-publishing to cooking. Some of the minuses of cooking are obvious—the time, the skills to learn, perhaps no talent or familiarity, and of course, the cleaning up. But with time and interest you get better and you start to see cooking as a lifelong passion and a constant challenge with immediate rewards.

Neither are inherently "good" or "bad," just different.

WHY I LOVE SELF-PUBLISHING

I'm so proud to be self-published today, and you should be, too. Your involvement, your control, your creativity, your rights and your royalties, where and how your book is sold, what editions you release, they are all up to you.

In fact, here are 14 reasons I *love* and am *proud to be* in self-publishing:

1. General self-reliance

2. Complete creative control

3. Realtime business data

4. Proven paths to success

5. As public or as private as you want to be

6. Self-actualization

7. Unlimited income

8. Big Publishing no longer controls what information we have

9. Zero required schedules and appointments

10. Work when and how and where you want

11. Perpetual challenges, learning, and awakenings

12. The most direct relationships with readers

13. It takes some courage and some stepping out of the box, and many never do

14. A constant sense of accomplishment

THE RISE OF SELF-PUBLISHING

So let's really get started. I consider the four most useful self-publishing platforms today to be:

- Kindle Direct Publishing (KDP)

- IngramSpark (IS)

- Draft2Digital (D2D)

- Lulu (LL)

I'll only focus on these for now, as some or all combined will likely make up your publishing (or *distribution*) strategy, but know that others exist, and as niches reveal themselves in the market, more evolution will take place, giants might fall (history proves they do), and new ones are likely to rise.

There are other publishing platforms and services, some large, some boutique, that offer things the above do not, such as special edition and leatherbound books, more binding options such as spiral bound and saddle stitch, foil detail on covers, and so on. But for now we'll focus on those you are most likely to use today.

INGRAMSPARK (IS)

They were closed, but we stopped by anyway. Book Geek :)

Let's start with IngramSpark[28], which is the self-publishing subdivision of Ingram Content Group. More than 50 years ago[29], long before the advent of the Internet or digital publishing, it's probable that when we picked up a paperback at Waldenbooks in the mall (who remembers?), it was written by an author who wrote a book, sent a query letter and got a positive response from a publisher in New York City, got a publishing deal, and had one of the Big Six (now Big Five) publishers edit, design, plan a launch, and invest $ in both promotion and a print run of books based on their confidence in sales through the end of a launch week. (Interesting, I understand the print run of Hemingway's first book was about 5,000 copies, and his next 50,000.) If the book "paid out," or earned back what they laid out as an advance to the author

---

[28] https://www.ingramspark.com/
[29] https://www.ingramcontent.com/about

and the cost of the initial run, they might continue their interest in that author and their book(s).

So even before the digital revolution Ingram was producing, printing, and distributing books all over the world—a *very different* world, perhaps. For this reason I compare Ingram to Rome, as "all roads lead there," and have been there a very long time. Ingram's greatest asset today, as far as I can see, is it has long-established and wide-reaching *distribution channels—39,000 retail outlets*, in fact. They do this by taking the information and files you upload to IngramSpark and place your title (book) as a listing in various *wholesale catalogs* (such as Baker & Taylor), which are then perused by brick-and-mortar and online bookstores who get their inventory or sell directly from them.

Getting Into Bookstores

So, Ingram is the place to get your book into bookstores, but it has to be set up "right," and that means you choose to make your book "returnable" *by bookstores* and to offer an acceptable *discount to the trade* for your book. If you set your book up "right" with IngramSpark, you can walk into a Barnes & Noble and ask to hold a book signing there. Do this! Even if you have friends and family form a line, get video and pictures! It's a milestone in a life, and it's marketing gold. The clerk will likely look your book up in their system and see that it's set up as they require, and agree to hold a book signing with you there in the store. Cool, right?

Again, setting your book up "right" means you have a full listing created and meet all required file specifications, but in particular have set up *returnability* and a *trade discount* which bookstores require.

RETURNABILITY

Returnability is allowing *bookstores* (not shoppers) to return books *to you, the publisher,* which they have been unable to sell. Many bookstores will try a new title by buying maybe five copies for the shelf, *but shelf space in a bookstore is very valuable real estate* and if the books don't "move," they will want to send a few back. In fact they're used to sending books back to the publisher if they can't sell them.

I set books up as returnable during the file and data upload steps with IngramSpark, and opt to have them shipped back to the author at wholesale cost plus shipping, rather than destroyed. More on this in the "Distribution" step of the Book Creation Cycle detailed in Book 2, but for now also know that this is normal, that bookstores *won't* carry your book if it is not returnable or if it does not offer enough margin (trade discount).

Also know that in 13 years I have not had any serious issues with returnability except once. Usually, you'll find a package at your door out of the blue with one to three copies of your book and no real explanation other than a hard-to-understand "statement" from Ingram. No big deal—they cost you slightly more than wholesale, and you now have three more copies on hand. But once, a great client and friend had set up three book signings at her local Barnes & Nobles. The stores all ordered copies for the signings and then COVID and a medical issue with her father hit, so she of course had to cancel the appearances. In total, about a hundred copies of her book were then returned and she faced around a $1,000 invoice from Ingram. We worked that out, of course, but it's only been a problem, really, that one time in 13 years.

TRADE DISCOUNT

Ingram highly recommends your discount to the trade be 55 percent, so if you set your retail price at $10, bookstores can buy it wholesale for $4.50 and you make the remainder minus fees, but I have found in practice and from a book distributor (who services airports) that they very often accept books at a lower trade discount of 40 percent. (*Thank me later,* and not sure about lower than that, yet.) This has been very important to find out as it means a lot for self-published authors, especially with tight margins, particularly with hardcover and color interior books as they are costlier to produce.

"39,000 RETAIL OUTLETS"

Another thing to know is Ingram states they reach something like "over 40,000 retail channels" with your book. Awesome. Ingram is *the* distribution channel for print books, period. So much so that when you upload a book to KDP or Lulu and just about any other *print* platform, there is a check box for "Expanded Distribution." With KDP, that means if you'd like your book on sites other than Amazon they will run your book through *their own (KDP's) Ingram account.* If we get you published with IngramSpark we do *not* check "Expanded Distribution" in KDP. In fact, distributing your book with both Ingram and KDP Expanded Distribution can cause an "ISBN conflict" because the same ISBN will be put through one's own IngramSpark (IS) account as well as through KDP Expanded Distribution, or KDP's Ingram account.

So, why opt for Expanded Distribution with KDP when also going directly through Ingram? Same with Lulu and probably any platform that makes the claim of "40,000 retail outlets." Important because many strategies I recommend include using multiple publishing platforms.

TYPES OF DISTRIBUTION

For clarity—and you know how I love to define terms—let's pause a second and make clear the *types of distribution* we talk about as indies:

"DISTRIBUTION"

Distribution is simply the act of getting your book (comprised of data and files) *out there* to retail channels where it can be sold. In the Book Creation Cycle a whole step is devoted to "Distribution," and that simply means we've gotten our files and our data ready and then fill in all the blanks and upload our files to a *distribution platform* like KDP or Ingram.

"EXPANDED" OR "WIDE DISTRIBUTION"

Expanded or wide distribution simply means distribution to more than one channel, and thus, *wide* distribution. Now, remember, while perhaps all books should eventually receive wide distribution, there are times and places for different *distribution strategies*. For example, I came up with a launch plan I called the "Amazon 90," which is a distribution strategy where we publish exclusively to Amazon for 90 days and then likely add wide distribution (unless we kicked butt with Amazon alone those first 90 days). Part of the reasoning there is to concentrate all initial sales through Amazon to maximize rank and hopefully reviews in that first 90 days before moving on to include other sales channels.

The term "Expanded Distribution" comes from Kindle Direct Publishing. When you set your book's price, there's a checkbox for "Expanded Distribution." It means you want Kindle to send your book out to channels *other than* Amazon. And again, guess how they do that? *Kindle has an account with Ingram.* So if you plan to *never* use Ingram you *might* check that box but I *generally* recommend leaving it unchecked, and:

- Publishing an eBook and a paperback with KDP

- Going wide by publishing an additional paperback and a hardcover with Ingram

- And I'm now recommending Draft2Digital for your eBook's wide distribution outside of Amazon.

"FULL SERVICE DISTRIBUTION"

Full service distribution means your book is being actively promoted and pushed out *in print format to brick and mortar bookstores.* This is something a traditional or perhaps a hybrid publisher does for you, or you can do for yourself as an indie. Publishers also sometimes have relationships with bookstores where they recommend what books the store carries. Again, when a publisher claims they will get you "in" 39,000 or 40,000 retail outlets, it just means they have an Ingram account. It *does not mean* they will get your physical book placed in those stores—that's, again, called "full service distribution." You can accomplish as much directly with your own Ingram account.

Ingram is my preferred platform for all print editions because of the awesome *wide distribution* and the many print options they offer (paperback and various types of hardcover, including jacketed). It was originally intended for publishers large and small, so their interface is not as user-friendly as newer companies' (like Kindle Direct Publishing, Lulu, and Draft2Digital), and their reporting has been a historic pain in the ass, although they have recently much improved it (even if we still cannot tell *what stores* your sales are coming from).

Lastly, for now anyway, on Ingram, they used to charge fees—$49 per book plus re-upload fees of $25 if you uploaded new files at any time. They recently did away with them completely. This, I think, is a BIG deal, probably a BIG transition for Ingram, and I hope it pays off in droves :)

NO MORE BOOK SETUP FEES
IngramSpark

We believe that *all* authors should be able to successfully print, globally distribute and *Share Their Story With the World!* In our tenth anniversary year, we're announcing exciting changes that will make publishing your book with IngramSpark even easier.

No more book setup fees (Coming May 1st)
We will no longer charge book setup fees. It's that simple. Upload your books for free*.

I love IngramSpark. I was excited to learn the platform 13 years ago as a neophyte because I was excited to produce hardcover books and see books I worked on in places other than Amazon. I have always been eager to learn new facets of the publishing business. I can imagine heated discussions in the Ingram boardroom since Amazon decided to drop bombs on their business model and put pressures on them to compete in perhaps unexpected ways. They've faltered, here and there, too, from my view, in the last few years with color-interior book printing and with silly shipping mistakes. But to be fair, they *dominate print production and wide distribution of print titles.*

Ingram made it possible for little 'ole me to publish jacketed hardcover books and see them in Barnes & Noble, and they've enabled my clients to do book signings and all sorts of cool things only possible to a snobby elite in the past.

Thank you, IngramSpark!

I bet Ingram has also had a few sleepless nights over rising print and shipping costs, and by the plague of failing brick and mortar bookshops (which I hate, although Mom and Pop bookshops seem to be on the rise, and there's still IndieBound[30]). My hope for Ingram is they stick to their strengths and not get watered down trying to beat other platforms at their respective games.

For example, I no longer recommend Ingram for ebooks, (or "eBooks") only because others do it better. For example, Draft2Digital gives you so many more options for your ebook, such as coupons, perma-free ebooks, and other promotional

---

[30] https://www.indiebound.org/

opportunities. And I find it beneficial to also publish your ebook and paperback with KDP as there are advantages.

KINDLE DIRECT PUBLISHING (KDP)[31]

Amazon is killing a lot of good in the world, like bookstores and local commerce in general, but there's no reason we can't start shopping local more, and that includes bookstores, if and when they appear. Just as much, Amazon has disrupted publishing in so many good ways. I would not be what I am today without digital publishing, print-on-demand, and self-publishing. After all, *books* is where I needed to be, even if I knew it early on (I knew in college) and even if, for reasons, writing seemed like an impossible dream back then.

So I'm especially grateful to Amazon, and perhaps it was meant to be since my early sales efforts, failed small businesses, collapsed house as a real estate investor, bad ideas for innovation in real estate brokerage (I mortgaged my house and opened an office in an expensive shopping mall), later sales efforts (cookware demonstrations at home shows), and rock drumming didn't pan out. In fact, after the real estate bubble burst, before I had a toehold in writing, looking to feed my young family, I was turned down for a waiter job at our local Carrabba's, as if the applying wasn't pride-swallowing enough. I waited tables and loved it and learned a lot over many years but didn't plan to go back.

And now that I think about it, what scares me even more is the idea of sticking with the businesses that *did* seem to work out, at least for a while—our flea market shop, my tile

---

[31] https://kdp.amazon.com/en_US/

business, being a real estate agent, broker, and office manager. While all really good, satisfying memories, and invaluable experiences, *this—books—is where I was meant to be.* Maybe somebody upstairs has been, in ways, looking out for me! Maybe they even slapped their heads as they slapped me back to where I was meant to be. But here I am, and after 13 years, *I still love what I do.*

So, thank you, Amazon!

As far back as the 1970s the seeds of digital publishing began to sprout[32]. I remember the term "desktop publishing," and early, groundbreaking software like Microsoft Publisher (1991) and Adobe InDesign (1999), which brought publishing to your home computer. Along came Amazon in 1994[33], and the first Kindle e-reader in 2007[34], just three years before I jumped into freelance writing and publishing books on Amazon in 2010. *Exciting!* Whether I knew it at the time or not, Amazon planned to take over the world.

Even today, Amazon seems to be a story of acquisitions and exclusivity, whether achieved by actual agreed-upon exclusivity or by sheer dominance. Look at the results today. It's hard to buy books without Amazon, and I've tried. And selling books? I think too many rely too much on Amazon, but much more on that in *Book 3, Exponential Author Growth.*

When I started in 2010, Amazon had already coined the now-generic term "Kindle" to mean "ebook" (or as Amazon likes to spell it, "eBook"). And my first jump into things was again, with this little partnership out of Australia which sold a marketing package that included "publishing a book" to

[32] https://en.wikipedia.org/wiki/Electronic_publishing
[33] https://en.wikipedia.org/wiki/Amazon_(company)
[34] https://en.wikipedia.org/wiki/Amazon_Kindle

establish one's expertise. It was a state-of-the-art approach to marketing at the time, and it's persisted through today, with only slight changes from that business-focused niche. But back then it was *exciting* for me, and somehow, it still is—publishing, that is.

The book included in that marketing package was conceived by the partners to mean:

A. Finding a cheap writer on Elance and having them write a 20,000-word book on the client's subject matter for about $150 (ouch).

B. The managing partner would then quickly format the ebook and publish it on Amazon. I think she also did the front covers at first, if I remember right.

I came along and jumped into this, writing *lots* of books for them. I formed a great relationship with the managing partner, who started asking me to review what other writers had done and fix them as needed, if possible, and in cases re-doing what they'd done. By that point she had become a bit overwhelmed with the work as she was managing customers, researching metadata, hiring and managing writers, doing all the uploads to Kindle, dealing with customer complaints, and everything else I am probably unaware she had on her plate.

I was eager to learn how to do the uploads and other facets of self-publishing with Amazon, which for ebooks included a JPG (photograph-friendly) file for your front cover, and a Word file for your interior. Formatting for ebook interiors was uber-simple—It's still limited, as you are usually providing *reflowable* content that will be displayed according to the reader's preferences, so the design options are few in order to remain flexible and work on different devices, even within the Kindle line of readers.

But I got to cut my teeth on writing for experts, writing research-based non-fiction, and I learned how to find and preserve an author's voice, as a slew of their customers came from the National Speaker's Association. I had also been invited (thrust) into editing, and I was eager to expand what we did to include print editions, which the managing partner didn't mind me doing. I think the lead partner would have objected, but she saw how adding print editions would help *her* as they could deliver more value.

So, I was still limited to the world of Kindle Direct Publishing (KDP), and back then the print platform for paperbacks was a company called CreateSpace[35], which Amazon acquired in 2005, five years before I started freelance writing. CreateSpace had its own website where you'd upload a different set of files—a PDF for your interior (which allowed for full interior book design) and a PDF for your full cover (back + spine + front) for your paperback. I'd design the interiors in Word and convert them to PDF files. I'd design the covers in Paint Shop Pro (because I couldn't afford the industry-standard Photoshop back then, which was something like $700 to $1,000, and no pay-as-you-go program yet available as it is today with Adobe Creative Cloud), and then convert (or "export") the cover files to PDF as well.

We were now producing paperbacks. I was thrilled, and in 2010, I was becoming a page and cover designer as well as a writer and editor. Very cool. But I wanted more, I wanted to learn hardcover production, and we added Lightning Source, which is now IngramSpark.

---

[35] On-Demand Publishing, LLC, doing business as CreateSpace, is a self-publishing service owned by Amazon. The company was founded in 2000 in South Carolina as BookSurge and was acquired by Amazon in 2005. — https://en.wikipedia.org/wiki/CreateSpace

Along the way, a few notable experiences with Kindle included the *great reviews debacle* of about 2012 or so. The platform Fiverr had gotten rolling, and the managing partner looked there for cheap (often $5), basic cover designs. Well, just as the partners were somewhat violently splitting up, the managing partner was using Fiverr for paid reviews on Amazon—fake reviews to get clients quickly up to five or ten reviews on their books. But Amazon started cracking down on reviews, and kudos! because reviews being organic, honest, and as they like to say, *useful* is vital to the platform. In fact, back then an old friend asked me to leave a review on one of his products (not a book) and I said no. Amazon started removing reviews and in cases closing publishing accounts for posting paid or fake reviews.

Real reviews are vital. Actual, reliable social proof is a great benefit of online platforms like Amazon. Lose that, and close shop, really. And today, Amazon seems just as vigilant about making sure the reviews are as genuine as they can keep them. Bravo. I learned then how Amazon's *terms of service* was vitally important, or, as important as your publishing account was to you. It's their proprietary playing field, and these are their terms. Violate them and find another playing field, which stinks when Amazon is occupying 85 percent or so of the ebook market.

There was also a period where Amazon was said to test brick-and-mortar bookshops, but these seem limited today to being found in grocery stores[36]. They also announced testing drone delivery, which seems to still be a beta and limited to two locations[37]. The Sprinter vans have worked, wildly, of course. We now see them everywhere, every day. One author-client's husband runs an Amazon delivery service with a small

---

[36] https://www.amazon.com/find-your-store/

[37] https://www.amazon.com/gp/help/customer/display.html?nodeId=T3jxhuvPfQ629BOIL4

fleet of vans, so I'd hear inside info from them from time-to-time on what it was like contracting with Amazon.

Along the way Amazon folded CreateSpace into the KDP platform, which seemed like about a six-month transition. It was bumpy, but now it's great. Now, with both paperback and eBook format available in one place (KDP) it's very easy. You upload one edition (such as your ebook), and then simply add the appropriate files and price to have another edition (such as paperback), both already associated/attached within KDP.

In the last few years there has been an ongoing beta test for hardcovers within KDP. I think it's interesting that KDP has not moved further with them. At this writing, they still offer them as a third option/edition, but the available trim sizes are very few, and the page count has to exceed 75. For that reason and others (like wide distribution) we still look to Ingram as the place for hardcovers, as they get distributed to Amazon anyway. I'm surprised Amazon has not lowered the page count requirement yet and added a few more available trim sizes (like landscape and square) because they'd instantly be in children's books. Time will tell. I can only imagine what goes on internally with such decisions.

It's been very interesting to watch the performance of Support with both KDP and IS through the years, and it's something to be aware of. Ingram used to be harder to deal with, requiring an outside email from the address of the account holder, longer wait times, and often inadequate answers, but they've *much* improved. Interactions with Support in either platform depend on the experience of the team member you draw. With Kindle Support you almost always get a response within 24 hours, but the quality depends again, on who helps you. Patience with new people goes a long way, as does a dash of gratitude.

It can be interesting to get info from other quarters that might explain what you're experiencing with the different platforms. For example, just as I was having clients report sort of newbie responses from KDP Support, one author-client told me Amazon had just laid off about 4,000 people. Then, my brother-in-law who worked remotely for Amazon was told he'd have to start showing up to an office, which now means he has to move to either Virginia or Texas and leave Florida.

To be fair, support from both platforms has historically been very helpful, even if a response is alarming at first, from time-to-time.

Too many writers leave all their eggs in the Amazon basket. With only a few exceptions, perhaps for romance and sci-fi authors currently kicking butt in Kindle Select, you should publish wide if you're serious about your book(s). Not all giants last, or last as they are. My personal opinion is a whole bunch of decentralization is on the way. And as the legendary hockey quote goes …

> "I skate to where the puck is going to be,
> not where it has been."
> —WAYNE GRETZKY

GAINS & PAINS

I hope these insights make both KDP and IS platforms seem more familiar. Many treat them like frightful gods, but they're all *partners*. In fact, now without any fees from either, *they only make money when we make money.* I hope in some way these anecdotes make sense of how they behave now and in the future, and I hope you, as a modern author, now have a wider vision that includes the possibility of new platforms rising, possibly as old ones falter. That will probably come in the form of mergers and acquisitions, as we just saw with

Smashwords being acquired by Draft2Digital. While I'm a big fan of de-centralization in general, I think this particular example of *strategic growth* in this case is good for us as indies. Smashwords and Draft2Digital are both eBook platform pioneers that have brought us more options. As indies, ebooks are our bread and butter. And by merging (or the acquisition of Smashwords) Draft2Digital is now bigger and stronger, presumably creating more competition for Amazon—in fact the merger caused me to stop using Ingram for eBooks almost altogether. It's a good example of how the industry can evolve over a 13-year period.

And hopefully, in the new world, our maps will be peppered with Mom and Pop bookshops, ideally with great espresso and jazz. (I had an idea you can run with, of opening bookshops called *salons* that offer *sanctuary,* new and used books, readings, classes, great/local baked goods, and of course, kick-ass coffee.)

A few thoughts at this point on self-publishing and where we are, first, though:

The good:

- Anyone can publish a book, and with guidance, publish to *professional standards.*

- Making a career as an author is now hard work and hard science, rather than by the grace (and biases) of New York publishing houses.

- Authors now make *more* per-book than in the past, when an author would get about a buck a copy. I have to explain this all the time to clients who get shocked they might only make a few dollars on their book, per copy.

- While most seem to think "people don't read anymore," I'm convinced *more* people are reading *than ever before. Millions* of books are now published every year—I remember when we all watched that exceed one million—and I think that applies to just ebooks and print books, not sure if that *million* includes *audiobooks.*

Amazon and others are great equalizers, and have created a level playing field for all wanna-be and established authors. The fact of more books than ever being professionally (well) produced by so many, with new forms of writing and reading, with the fact that "a high tide raises all boats" (the more worthy books the better for the civilization), I think we're headed for or perhaps already in a Golden Age of Books.

The biggest casualty in all of this so far, if you ask me, is *Where have all the bookstores gone?* We should support the ones that pop up. It's a hard business these days.

DRAFT2DIGITAL (D2D)

To be honest, I have very little experience with Smashwords[38] and Draft2Digital[39], but I am now recommending Draft2Digital as the standard platform for wide distribution of ebooks, as mentioned. This is because I find IngramSpark to be the platform of choice for wide print distribution, KDP excellent for ebook and paperback distribution to Amazon, and Draft2Digital for the options, opportunities, and really great, wide distribution of ebooks.

---

[38] https://www.smashwords.com/
[39] https://www.draft2digital.com/

Years ago I found Smashwords and Draft2Digital as ebook distribution and sale platforms, but for my purposes, they didn't seem necessary. I used both KDP and IS for ebook distribution right up to recently, and have always tried to keep an author's number of platforms to as few as possible. In fact, I wondered why an author might use Smashwords or Draft2Digital, and imagined it was for wide distribution for authors *not creating print editions* with Ingram. Or for those self-published authors in genres that do really well specifically with ebooks, such as science fiction and romance, which have voracious readers. Some authors in these genres don't see a need for the time and expense of creating print editions when their ebooks sell as they do. They'd rather spend their time *writing more books,* which is paramount, of course.

I was aware they offered wide distribution and perma-free books, meaning you could make an ebook *permanently free,* very useful for the first book of a series or for "baits" (other, short books you make permanently free to connect with new readers). You can't set up books as permanently free on KDP (Amazon), although there used to be ploy where you'd make your ebook perma-free through D2D, then find the "Find this book cheaper?" button on your Amazon book's page and report it was free on other platforms. Amazon used to then make your ebook free without being enrolled in Select, which was valuable, again, at the start of a series. (Free books historically do not seem to help you get reviews, by the way, but more on that when we discuss reviews.) This ploy doesn't seem to work as well, lately.

Smashwords and Draft2Digital offered checklist distribution, where you pick the channels you distribute to, and you can distribute to Amazon as one of your choices, so you can bypass using KDP altogether if you wish. I try to set clients up on the simplest approach, with the fewest platforms as possible. And as mentioned, with D2D there are options not available with KDP such as coupons.

Today, the trio of IS, KDP, and D2D (Kindle Direct Publishing, IngramSpark, Draft2Digital) is wonderful. You have a wealth of options with all of the above, and can create, as a modern author, a distribution strategy that rivals and really, exceeds what many publishers might set you up with. You have wide distribution and complete control with real-time data to work with and no go-betweens or bottlenecks, either.

We call it "self-publishing." :)

Quick note: Some publishers and self-publishing consultants/companies still set you up either on KDP alone or with KDP and IS, but if so, your ebook might be missing out in many ways. *It's ultimately up to you, as a modern author, to know your options. It's you, after all, who will live with your book for the rest of your life.*

I have to give a shout out to Mark Coker, the founder of Smashwords, who did a beautiful job with the company for many years and created an incredibly valuable podcast called "The Smart Author[40]." I learned *gobs* from it, including the value of a preorder period and the opportunities we sometimes overlook with libraries. They had an annual marketing report[41] ("survey") that was intensely interesting for self-published authors I always looked forward to. Mark recently sold Smashwords to Draft2Digital, and the rest is history.

---

[40] https://www.smashwords.com/podcast
[41] https://blog.smashwords.com/

LULU

Like Kindle Direct Publishing (KDP) and IngramSpark (IS), Lulu is another online book production and distribution platform. They have their own online bookstore. They cater to authors who want ways to sell their books directly from their websites. They offer lots of choices in book trim sizes and binding types. But they distribute *through Ingram,* so I only use Lulu for special situations.

It's actually a bit funny, if accurate, how my view of Lulu has evolved over 13 years. When I was starting out and looking into platforms more, Lulu was there, but the word was their print quality was generally poor. I didn't know if that was even true or not, but I had KDP and IS, and really didn't need another option, so never really used Lulu back then.

A few years later I was hired to create a *legacy book,* interviewing several generations of family members and stitching it together into a narrative nonfiction book for the family alone. The client's assistant researched and found that with Lulu you could print books *without* distributing them for retail availability. (Ingram recently added the ability to create a print book just for your own purchasing, rather than distributing it.) And I started working with Lulu, for the first time, really. If it was true that they had quality issues, they might have over-corrected because today I find the most consistent high quality in print and shipping coming from Lulu. I've even had a client order her same book from both Lulu and the others and compare them, and found not only what seemed like thicker paper, but more vibrant colors. Fascinating! The thing is, like KDP, Lulu uses Ingram's distribution network (they both have accounts with Ingram to tap into the distribution network), so if you're publishing with IS already I don't think you need Lulu.

So, when do you need Lulu?

With another client about two years ago, we found Lulu offered a way to sell your book from your website using the Lulu Express app within Shopify. So when people buy your book from your website, if you have things set up with a $9 per month "buy button" from Shopify, Lulu fulfills the orders for you *and you capture buyer information and can grow your email list,* which you can't do with sales from most retail platforms like Amazon or with books sold through Ingram. Brilliant! Today they have Lulu Direct to make it easy to sell and fulfill orders right from your website.

With another client just in the last month, we were getting a bit close for comfort on having a print order delivered in time for a special event. I uploaded their book to KDP, IS, D2D, and Lulu just because Lulu is very print-only friendly, meaning, as discussed, you don't have to *distribute,* you can create a book there solely for your own printing. And with Lulu, you can place your print order immediately upon uploading your files, whereas with KDP and IS your book goes though up to a 72-hour final approval process before you can order copies. Their order of about 40 books arrived with a week to spare, and the print quality was great.

I'll be doing more with Lulu soon, as when this book and the next (*Book 2: The Book Creation Cycle*) are done, I'm going to work out and test many ways to sell books directly for greater profit, so authors can become *viable* authors more quickly. And the results will be shared in the third in the series, *Book 3: Exponential Author Growth.*

Thank you, Lulu!

A final note: Lulu is more than books. They have what they call "Lulu Express" which is their platform for *only* books, not to get confused with the more general Lulu (as I was at first). The bigger Lulu is like a VistaPrint with books and all kinds of products, and they've found a niche for options you don't find with KDP and IS, such as coil and saddle stitch binding, and more. And selling directly is *important* for self-published authors who are growing an email database, which you simply cannot do with books through KDP or IS.

OTHER PLATFORMS

There are and will continue to be more ways to publish, some established and growing, some new to me, and some arriving all the time. Worth knowing, or at least keeping an eye open for, because what if Amazon goes under? Or Ingram? I know it seems like they'll be around forever, but so did that buggy-whip company about a hundred years ago, so did MySpace seem invincible. And even if they don't die a sudden or grandiose death, many social media platforms, for example, in recent years have taken *political stands* and committed unapologetic *censorship,* lost pounds of flesh, and that might or might not affect you and your livelihood. As I write this *big companies* are going into bankruptcy as the whole world is changing the way we do business. But *life will find a way.* There will be new ways to share information and publish books, just watch the horizon. If you can predict things even a little bit you can save yourself periods of starvation.

The other known negative is what's called a *slap,* where a sudden change in policy crashes an author's living overnight. It's happened a few times in my 13 years, on Amazon alone, once with reviews, and once with "Also Boughts[42]," where Amazon would recommend your book (for free) below

---

[42] https://davidgaughran.com/also-boughts-amazon-recommendations/

relevant search results. Many authors relied upon this heavily, and once gone and requiring payment (if you could still get it), it created a crisis for more than one author who had to build back *quickly.*

That's not to say nothing good happens! At least as far as we authors are concerned. Audiobooks has opened wide for us, which is great, and is the fastest growing segment of publishing at this writing. Ingram dropped all fees. Draft2Digital gets more powerful, which is great for indies. I'm excited about what I hope is coming and just as excited by what *I know I do not know* is coming! It's an exciting business. Dynamic.

Diversification is assumed to mean publishing wide for the modern author, but it can also mean keeping your options open, even to alternative platforms. I keep an eye open and make a note when I find them, and sometimes reach out and arrange to meet specialty service providers. As mentioned, I've had clients ask or tell me about providers of leatherbound and other special editions available for the (modern) self-published author. Here are a few I'm aware of:

- Vervante: https://www.vervante.com/

- WhiteFox: https://www.wearewhitefox.com/

- And don't forget about the special stuff Lulu offers.

Publishing Direct

If you are a full-time author or publisher, you might also look into publishing *directly* with the prominent retail outlets. I tried this not too long ago by publishing directly with Barnes & Noble Press and iBooks, for example. We were acting on a strategy I formed for achieving a *national best seller* (remember that term) with *USA Today* by strategically promoting and releasing our book through specific distribution channels at strategic times through a preorder period.

Some sales channels do not aggregate preorders and some do, reporting accumulated sales all on launch day. And the understanding is *USA Today* wants to see sales across multiple platforms. So, we'd make the book available one platform at a time until we met certain preorder milestones.

By "kicking out the middleman" (in this case Ingram and Draft2Digital) and publishing direct with iBooks and Barnes & Noble Press I also hoped to improve per-book sales margins. I also thought each platform would offer its own ways to promote within the channel and wanted to test them.

It didn't work. The finickiness of the individual platforms was a genuine pain in the ass, which surprised me because I know the requirements for KDP and IS and Lulu and a few others like the back of my hand. I learned even if they are a prominent retail sales channel, that doesn't mean they cater directly to self-published authors or have much experience or investment in their platforms or processes. It was a disaster.

It made me appreciate the convenience of publishing with distribution platforms like IS, KDP, and D2D. These have figured out the requirements for *all* retail platforms and make life much easier. They keep things all in one place (or three places) for you, even if they extract a small percentage for the favor. Plus your reporting will be in fewer places. In fact, I've had at least two clients recently reach me for help in *getting rid of a platform,* or moving everything over to just one.

So, while I suggest using the prominent platforms like IS, KDP, and D2D, I first suggest:

A. Arranging to sell books directly from your website or in live events

B. Then worry about optimizing whatever is the predominant channel of the day (currently Amazon)

C. And test a niche sales channel, depending on your genre.

If you start with those *three sales channels* you can learn a lot and not have things get out of control at first. You can also start building an email list of readers and maximize margins.

An expert, experienced traditional publisher once explained to me that you usually cannot tell where your book will do better. There is no simple "Romance does best in iBooks," for example. He suggested it's simply a matter of testing.

And if I had to choose a single platform it would be IngramSpark. You can distribute to all channels, including Amazon, in all formats—ebook, paperback, and hardcover.

BOOK DISTRIBUTORS

A *book distributor,* or one definition of that, is that dude or dudess who you see hurriedly (probably so you won't bother them) placing and organizing books and magazines on the racks at the airport shop (usually a Hudson's) or hospital. Some shops have a book distributor who periodically (see what I did there?) comes in and takes away the old magazines and slow-to-sell books and replaces them with new magazines and books they hope will sell better. I have tried chasing down book distributors and corporate offices to get my and clients' books carried, to no avail so far, but close. The effort became a matter of diminishing returns, and I think this is why many self-published authors do not pursue these channels often, if at all. But, the channel (airports, hospitals) is there, you know more about it now, and you can show up with your *book one sheet* and a few copies of your book in hand to give them. If you do try this let me know! I *might* pursue it again once the first two books in this series are published, as a test for *Book 3: Exponential Author Growth*.

PRINT LOCATIONS

The subject of "Where are my books printed?" is important once in a while. For example, it used to be KDP had no print facility in Australia, so my Australian clients had to have their print editions produced and distributed by Ingram or their readers might balk at high shipping costs from Amazon facilities in other countries.

I'm kicking myself because I saved at one time an excellent email from Ingram Support explaining clearly the printing facilities and so on, but it almost doesn't matter, as this seems to change often. KDP has added an Australian facility, for example, and I suspect publishing platforms farm out their printing to independent printers as well, but then need to stand behind the print quality, of course—an important consideration we'll get into more in *Book 3,* as we want to avoid becoming entangled in print quality issues if we start selling directly.

LOCAL PRINTERS

I hate to say this, as I'm a big fan and really believe the way of the future is smaller, local shops, but with few exceptions I have not had much luck with local printers. Not that they're not capable, but it's very hard to beat the wholesale prices you get with KDP, IS, and Lulu. And we've tried. One client had a great relationship with her printer in Australia, and that was a success, but when a client and I have gone about seeking them out, it's very hard to match or beat the prices on wholesale offered by the big boys.

DROP SHIPPING & WHOLESALE COPIES

Which reminds me, with your KDP, IS, and Lulu publishing accounts you have access to wholesale author print copies and the ability to drop ship to people. Otherwise, you can of course keep an inventory and ship from your garage or warehouse. Many authors do this with signed copies, and many keep a case of books in their trunk, or for selling directly at events and appearances.

SUMMARY

Modern publishing *rocks,* I mean, the business freedom, the creative freedom, the unlimited potential—and it's all hard science today. I believe *anyone,* even with a mediocre book, can find an audience. They're out there. Heck, if you paint yourself blue on weekends I'll bet there's a group for you, and today, *you can find them and form a tribe*. That's a definition of marketing, by the way.

Meanwhile, *congratulations* on getting this far. You are fast becoming a true modern author, and I hope we break rum at some point—maybe sooner than you think, see my podcast!

Next, let's take an important look at *what kind of book you hope to create*.

MODERN MEANINGS: WHAT ARE WE TALKING ABOUT, HERE?

"You keep using that word.
I do not think it means
what you think it means."

— INIGO MONTOYA (played by Mandy
Patinkin), from the movie, The Princess Bride

"INSTANT SPEED READING" (AND FOCUS)

A
S WRITERS, READING is fundamental. The ability to read quickly and clearly with comprehension has a lot to do with focus and familiarity, but we can "hack reading," as I found out on one fruitful occasion. If you have speed reading available as a tool when handy, it makes life

easier, but I think just the understanding that you can speed-read right now, improves your reading overall, and suggests there are *ways to read according to the occasion*. For example, when I do a manuscript review, I sort of speed-read (fast) and when I proofread I read aloud (or at least enunciate in my head and take my time, slowly).

Remember those old commercials for speed reading courses, where people had their heads buried in a book and ran their hand rapidly along the lines of a page? There's an easy way to get there. It also helps us understand what *reading is*. Words are symbols, packages of thought, you might say, that *represent a meaning*. But what if you bypassed that middle step, and rather than mechanically *thinking* in-between, simply went straight to the meaning? It takes a lot of focus, but that's the secret, *all you do is focus on meanings rather than words*.

- **Reading/literacy** = eyes on "spoon," *thinking* about the letters or saying "spoon" in your head, and then filling in the meaning, "spoon."

- **Speed-reading/super literacy** = eyes on "spoon," without thinking or enunciating the word in your head, simply understand "spoon"—don't think it or say it in your head, just take *meanings off the page*, like looking *through* the words.

Note that "diction" is your choice of words, and "tone" is how an author feels about their subject, which is often conveyed in the writing. Both can be still be appreciated with speed reading. It's just skipping the mechanical step that is *unnecessary* when you have distraction-free focus on *the meanings of the words rather than the words/symbols themselves.*

Electracy, remember? In fact the proof is also in symbols. You see a cross, a flag, and so on. They *represent* things to you.

Speed reading has a time and place. It's not "fun," perhaps, but useful, and cool. All those late-night TV people were doing was using their hands to focus. It works, too.

I desperately needed to finish a course I was taking where they hounded you like Nazis to progress and finish and exacted punishments on you if you failed to show. So it was important to me to finish, ASAP, and I figured my best way *out* was *through.* I pulled up to the building where the course was administered (everyone reading and writing on their own materials), and instead of going in, decided the only thing they would allow me to be late for was to be *finished,* which they always celebrated, so I went to my office a block away, sat down with the course materials, speed-read, answered the chapter questions, and walked in with the course completed after about 90 minutes. They loved me.

I say all this because (a) I bet you—or at least many of you—can speed read and you didn't know it, and (b) it relates not only to reading but also to the power of *focus.* It's part of my Word Count Triangle (discussed in *Book 2: The Book Creation Cycle,* in tips on productivity in writing), and it works to speed production—in fact, I believe good focus *improves* the *quality* of production and leads to *flow* as well, save those times we need ride out into the country or walk the beach to get a little more "30,000 feet" from our work and allow inspiration and bright ideas to show up. We most often see this in reverse, how we can't produce when not focused, but it works in the other direction, too. I'm sure you can think of examples from your own life.

Now to achieve focus, you normally need to ensure it's safe—the kids are safe, dinner is not in 20 minutes, there are no annoying noises—but you can achieve focus nonetheless. I once worked quite productively sitting on the floor of a crowded airport terminal. If the dude next to me could sleep, I decided I could work. This "focus factor" is part of the difficulty in shifting quickly from one writing project to another. (An artist/painter I met said the same thing, that switching projects without space between was one of the hardest things to do.) I like breaks in-between of some sort, especially mini-breaks of about five minutes. They work! But then again, maybe I'm lazy. Probably, actually. But I do know when I am focused—and things like quiet, no commitments, and espresso all help—I can write *a lot* and I usually enjoy it.

That night in my office, desperate to finish that damn course, in a quiet building, I simply *focused* on the *meanings* of the words as intended, alone or as small groups, scanning with the help of my hand at a pace where I found I could clearly understand what I was reading. Whenever I found myself thinking of anything other than the text I slapped myself back to focus on the *meanings not the words,* and voila, I was quickly assimilating the ideas in the book. I knew it was working because I could spot-test, I could read a paragraph and then look away and summarize it to myself, and understanding might be said to simply be *telling yourself.*

And, by the way, when we write books we are *telling ourselves,* so we increase our understanding, even of our own subjects which we are expert in!

Understanding words are simply representations of meaning, you can focus on strings of meaning, and you can speed read. Thank me later.

And you can look at a word and understand what it means *without sounding it out in your head*, but no one trains us to do this.

My intention here is simply to share that I believe we "self-enunciate" when reading not for comprehension but for focus, and thus, if you can gather enough focus as you read (look over words) you don't need to self-enunciate. It's often called *speed reading* or *super-literacy*, and I share it because some of you will get excited at the idea of reading *more in less time* and with complete comprehension.

"Semiotics"

I first understood "semiotics" to be the meanings we associate with colors, but it's more. When you look at a word you are flooded with anything from nothing at all (not familiar with a word, for example) to *loads* of meaning. In cover design especially, when someone sees your book cover as a thumbnail on Amazon, we have a millisecond to capture their interest enough that they, on some level, decide to keep their eye on your book page. If we pause here (we'll discuss this microprocess more when we talk about cover design and marketing basics in Book 2), we want our target reader to both:

A. Feel like they know what your cover is saying (through colors, emblems, images, title, especially)

B. And have a sense of mystery that sucks them in, at least enough they take the next micro-step of considering your subtitle or wherever they move their eye to next (an image, your name, a review, and so on).

This is part of the skill of marketing. Again, as Ulmer stated, "communicating at light-speed is done by means of emblems, slogans, mottos, logos (from Aristotle's logos to corporate logos).[43]" And for good measure, here's what Britannica says:

> "Semiotics, also called semiology, the study of signs and sign-using behaviour… 'something which stands to somebody for something,'… the categorization of signs into three main types:
>
> (1) an icon, which resembles its referent (such as a road sign for falling rocks);
>
> (2) an index, which is associated with its referent (as smoke is a sign of fire); and
>
> (3) a symbol, which is related to its referent only by convention (as with words or traffic signals).
>
> … a sign can never have a definite meaning, for the meaning must be continuously qualified."
>
> —https://www.britannica.com/science/semiotics

I include "semiotics" here because it's important to understand the meanings of things (not hard—the color red usually means stop, for example, and is known to "stop the eye") and the nuances as well (green=natural, blue=authority, etc.). I see too much bad design simply because the author or

---

[43] http://www.rhizomes.net/issue18/ulmer/index.html, accessed October 16, 2022

designer went outside the genre or used inappropriate colors. Sometimes just looking at your work *as a reader* is all you need to get a gut impression of what you've done, and can then decide if it's what you, *the writer,* intended.

The key to using similes and metaphors, by the way, is simply relevance and whether it adds or subtracts from your meaning. Metaphors and similes, semiotically speaking, can be efficient and powerful ways to imbue a text with meaning, emotion, even back story or inner psyche. For example:

> "You, of course, are a rose-
> But were always a rose."
>
> — ROBERT FROST, "THE ROSE FAMILY"

Now, watch how the meaning is destroyed with a bad, confusing, maybe even humorous metaphor:

> "You, of course, are a football-
> But were always a football."

Understand semiotics in your writing and in your design, in and on your book, and very much so in your marketing. It's part of being a savvy, modern author, because so much is done *for us, by us* these days. That's why we're called (affectionately) "indies," after all.

"WRITING"

Today, "writing," when it comes to writing books, means any means of getting thoughts from your head and from other sources into digital form so it can be manipulated and reproduced. What happens and who touches or handles it in-between doesn't really matter. This means if I interview you, you are the *author*, because they are your thoughts and/or your ideas, even if in that case I am the *writer,* and *we are both writing.*

I like to assure clients that no matter how they get their ideas and/or direction to me down—longhand, typing, dictation—they are *writing.* Sometimes it helps to know we're doing the right things and making progress in an acceptable way! Writing isn't just for pen and paper anymore, not if you're an *electrate, modern author.* The easiest we can make it and the more we validate whatever means works best for you to write, the more we help your process, which opens opportunities for the cognitions and often, catharsis, that come from a healthy process, and of course, the better a book we can create in good time.

And as we roll into "editing," it's worth mentioning that *your own communication can sound different when created by different means.* If I edit a book where we've created content from notes, author writings, and transcribed interviews, Once we have the content created and organized I will start smoothing the language so it all flows nicely. Kind of amazing. When Jessica worked with me we interviewed a client for his book. When we read the transcript individually, before meeting again with him, somehow it came up that the way he "sounded" in the transcript was *not him* as he "sounded" live on the phone. He sounded like a jerk in the transcript, but if you knew the client, he was a pussycat! The point is there can be a difference in language and tone given different recording mediums. The answer is familiarity with the voice we want, and *editing.*

"Editing"

I learned all about roofs when, as a beginning real estate investor in a previous life, I rounded up twelve bids on a roof I needed replaced. I mean, I talked to twelve roofers! In the same way, all the schooling in the world won't teach you what hiring an editor will. When I ran that small writing department and needed to find a few good editors, I posted a job on Elance (now Upwork). I provided a single paragraph I asked people to edit as a sample of their work, and wow, the differences in approach was expected, but the differences in *meaning* was a big surprise to me. Just by putting emphasis or slight changes in diction in different places (within *one* paragraph!) it made wholesale changes in what the paragraph actually seemed to say.

I also hired an editor once who edited *dialogue* for proper grammar, which is a big mistake! People don't speak "properly" (if there is such a thing).

So, editing is *as important as writing* (or only slightly less important, the writing being the ingredients, the editing the recipe, with both needed for a cake). We discuss it more later and in Book 2, but my mantra is "embrace editing," and you will, when you're done with this book series. You'll thank me, too.

> "I have made this longer than usual because I have not had time to make it shorter."
>
> —BLAISE PASCAL, French mathematician and philosopher, in a letter of 1657

It took me years to gain confidence as an editor, and I have it now. You have to understand your purpose, your genres, and then all the commonalities (or "rules" as they say). I have a philosophy of it for the books I typically work on:

> *Grammar works for us, to make things more recognizable and meanings clear. But we don't "serve it," it serves us.*

Embrace editing, but it's usually best to "write right through" your first draft, even if you simply add placeholders like <<crime scene>> to be filled in later, perhaps with the consultation of a detective, if that's the book. I've found some authors who edit as they go like it that way and put out great work, but I've met more who get stopped completely after a while, when they edit as they go. Big names like Stephen King recommend getting right through, first, then going on a two-week vacation while your editor takes things over until you get back.

And if you follow my Book Creation Cycle, there are plenty of chances for feedback and improvement of a draft, so no worries. And as mentioned, in my practice we only expand who sees your draft when it reaches certain stages. The result is a great book and a confident (modern) author.

In my practice we focus on *three* types or stages of editing:

1. **Developmental editing**: The 30,000-foot approach that considers overall organization, clarity, and flow of your book.

2. **Copy editing**: The line-by-line review that seeks *consistency* in grammar and corrects spelling, and might also pepper your book with footnotes and other additions if they *improve the read for the reader.*

3. **Proofreading**: Even editors miss things. Just read almost any published book, even those published by the Big Five New York publishers. So, a final pass before publishing is easily justified. Autocorrect alone can come behind you and change things.

If you do the above three and include a beta period where readers share their impressions before publishing, you'll be on par with any title out there in terms of professionally-prepared content. The modern author appreciates editing, as the best writers do. Some stick with their editors for many years once they find one they gel with. Professional-quality books depend on a high-quality editing process, and this was one of the ugly spots in the advent of self-publishing. Many self-published authors early on didn't edit their books at all, and it showed.

"Self-Publishing"

In the beginning, this kind of did mean you did everything yourself, and the results often reflected that. Traditional publishers initially flocked to malign the new practice. But today "self-publishers" hardly go it alone. In fact, rather than inherit a fixed team and subject yourself to "how things are done," you can learn best practices (which are in this book series), and either go it alone or assemble a dream team. Or you might simply contract out certain parts of the Book Creation Cycle, like cover design or editing.

In any case, you can now publish for yourself, and no longer need to be *by* yourself. In addition to a resource like this book series, there are many other books, blogs, videos, consultants, and I especially have come to like the social media groups where authors pose and solve for each other everything self-publishing.

Traditional publishers play a role today, of course, and always will, if you ask me, but "self-publishing" has removed *exclusivity of access* and replaced it with a level playing field. The doors to the "secret club" have been blown off by the Internet, print-on-demand, desktop/digital publishing, and by the sharing of best practices by generous influencers like Joanna Penn, David Gaughran, and others. The quality of self-published books has rapidly grown to usually meet or exceed those books put out by traditional publishers.

Self-publishing, in the last 13 years, has gone from ridiculed and feared, to a kind of Wild West, then grown and evolved, and now lands as a fully-qualified *profession*.

I gave a talk on stage in 2015 I called "The Secret of Self-Publishing." That secret was to *not look self-published.* So we'd make sure an author-client had a publishing name other than their own and a logo ("imprint"), that all the basics were in like a professional-looking cover and good editing, we'd publish in multiple formats, and so on. Well, that old taboo is all but gone today. In that time, Amanda Hocking self-published her way to a million-dollar traditional publishing deal for her young adult zombie stories (great, great article you should read linked in the footnote here[44]), and conversely, Mark Dawson left his traditional publisher for the total control over creativity and all things business self-publishing affords (another great, great article about self-publishing success linked in footnotes here[45]). But the real difference is the quality of self-published books now rivals or exceeds the quality of traditionally-published books. Period.

---

[44] https://www.theguardian.com/books/2012/jan/12/amanda-hocking-self-publishing

[45] https://www.forbes.com/sites/jaymcgregor/2015/04/17/mark-dawson-made-750000-from-self-published-amazon-books/?sh=482f7a236b5b

Today, you don't have to apologize, in fact you should be *proud* of being self-published. I always (yes, *always*) recommend self-publishing at least with your first book, unless perhaps if you are a household-name celebrity with a large following, and maybe a few other cases.

"INDIE"

A term of affection in the self-publishing community, simply meaning an independent/self-published author.

"PUBLISHER"

Okay, this is the juicy one. I think I can best explain with a little anecdote: A client I helped write, produce, and publish his book once said to me, "Rodney! A *publisher* is interested in my book!"

"That's great," I said. "Did he say if he needs any money up front?"

"Well, yes, I think so… He needs $6,000 up front, but he thinks I've written a great book!"

Well, maybe that's true.

We still, naturally, have an "ignorance gap." I'm old enough to still have the idea that a "publisher" and "publishing deal" involve a scene much like one from the movie, *Throw Momma from the Train,* where struggling writer Larry Donner's ex-wife hit's it big with her romance novel and gets a "publishing deal." She is sent on a book tour that includes champagne in an exotic suite in the tropics, a new boy toy, and presumably, a bunch of money. All while her "publisher" is doing all the heavy lifting for her, their newfound celebrity.

Perhaps that still exists, and we discussed "Types of Modern Publishers" earlier, in "Part I: Modern PUBLISHING," but you should know that "publisher" can mean one of many things today. Again, a simplified breakdown:

- **Traditional publishers** pay advances, get you on national media, push your book out to bookstores, and work to develop your career, all for a (large) share of rights and royalties.

- **Hybrid publishers** sometimes charge upfront or as-you-go fees, but set you up to whatever degree for success, and you then enjoy most or all of your rights and royalties.

- **Service publishers** simply do *work-for-hire* (as I do).

The problem I have, and the reason I called myself a collaborator and not a publisher all these years until recently, is I never wanted to exploit that ignorance gap by capitalizing on your sexy idea of what a publisher "is," because it's changed, clearly. But with these definitions alone you can know what the deal is, compare publishers, and choose what's best for you based on your own goals and resources. But in my mind, a "publisher" should have certain technical skills available to them, and be clear about their services, expectations, and terms. The good news is I now see far fewer snake oil salesmen and more and more competent, honest, and highly capable publishers, such as myself, such as others I know of, either from working with them or by familiarity over time. If ever I can't take a project, I'm always happy to recommend another provider.

Times change, reputations change, and thirteen years is apparently enough for me to watch publishers change their strategies, define their positions, and come and go. But hey, there has been a *lot* of creative disruption in the industry! Mostly for the good if you ask me, if more people are writing and publishing *worthy* books, because a high tide raises all boats.

"DISTRIBUTION"

I include "distribution" because it's a vital term to understand. Almost all clients don't know what it means at first, and it's sometimes used to exploit the ignorance gap. "Distribution" means getting your book out there to retailers. We do it in self-publishing by creating an account (or accounts) with the distribution *platform(s)* we choose and uploading our files, basically. The predominant platforms today, again, are:

- Kindle Direct Publishing (KDP)

- IngramSpark (IS)

- Draft2Digital (D2D)

If I had to recommend a *general* distribution strategy likely good for all or most authors, it would probably be using all three of the above, but we'll get deeper into that in this and other books in the series as it's an important strategic decision and I have different recommendations depending on your goals and situation. Each of these are at this writing established, "predominant" platforms (perhaps add Lulu to that as well), and each has its strengths, weaknesses, and time and place.

With these platforms and others, you can get your book listed with online retail book websites as well as in bookstores (if set up right). You can get your book in ebook and print form "on the shelf," so to speak. Now, getting published in ebook and print and in bookstores is an achievement in itself, but at that point you're still just a drop in the ocean. Remember, *millions* of books are now published each year. Once your book is live the real work begins, and if done right can be an exciting journey over time *out of* whatever you're trying to get out of and *into* a life and career as an author.

Where "distribution," or the idea of it, is abused, is when someone (and it's always "someone," as corporate entities don't really exist nor make decisions, but avoid liability) advertises they will "get you into over 40,000 retail outlets." (Up until recently it was "39,000.") While technically true, you'll be *available* to over 40,000 retail outlets just by being set up correctly with IngramSpark, but I'm sure there are those of us who read that to mean their book *will be physically placed* in over 40,000 retail outlets. Not so, and we have the same sort of bait-and-switch we have (less now than in the past) with terms like "publisher" and "best seller."

I once dug into one of the largest self-publishing company's packages on their website for a client and found they suggested a value of $900 for setting up "returnability." *And this is why this crap makes my blood boil.* "Returnability" is a single checkbox, basically, in the process of entering your data into IngramSpark's platform. It was a gross exaggeration of value to get your cash—*not "common marketing" as many might excuse or explain it.* Marketing is a profession, not a trick. Some outfits in these years have also made whole practices of guaranteeing to make you a "best seller," as discussed. How many, seeing these come-ons, have hopes of being flown to Hawaii, paid sacks of cash, with their book in both megastores and in the window of that little shop on Notting Hill, while checking the *New York Times* Best Seller List?

I'd rather have you a savvy, modern author with actual plans and actual success than burned in such a way. And we're not talking about being lied to over a carton of milk, *books are dreams for most people!*

I feel like I'm maybe being too dark here, so please keep in mind, there are pitfalls, and also, *your dreams of a great book or even becoming a full-time author are no longer dreams, they're science, and with the right guidance (from me and others) you can plan it and do it!*

By the way, self-published authors generally make most of their sales and income from ebooks, while traditionally-published authors typically make their bulk of sales and income from print books. You can accomplish both, you can even get your books in bookstores if you set them up correctly so you can work those print "channels" (we'll discuss *sales channels* including selling direct, and what I call *marketing tiers* for authors in depth *Book 3: Exponential Author Growth*) and even (rather easily) arrange book signings and get your books on endcaps in your local B&N.

"BOOK PROPOSAL"

Book proposals are used in traditional publishing to represent and sell your book to publishers. Think of them as part resume and part business plan for each book. In your book proposal you usually include a synopsis, a sample chapter, and research and findings on genre, target market, comparable books and authors, and ways to sell it. Traditionally, they can be as large as 50 pages and 50,000 words. One of my favorite authors, Erik Larson (*Dead Wake, The Devil in the White City*), who is beyond well-established, says he still prepares a full book proposal for each book.

But stick with me, I don't think you need one in long form. Today, there's a short-form version of about 1,500 words (as conceived by the bright minds at Publishizer.com), and for self-published authors they are very effective at kicking off and informing your marketing. But we're not seeking a traditional publisher, so what gives? *Always do a short-form book proposal, even if no one ever sees it. It will inform your marketing at first.* We'll discuss short-form book proposals in detail in *Book 2: The Book Creation Cycle,* in the marketing step. I think every author should start with a short-form book proposal as a first step in their marketing plans. They're actually fun and can be *very* enlightening.

"In the beginning was the Word,
and the Word was with God,
and the Word was God."

—JOHN 1:1,
New International Version Bible

PART II

ALL KINDS OF BOOKS

"You can find magic
wherever you look.
Sit back and relax,
all you need is a book."

— DR. SEUSS

AUDIOBOOKS

LET'S START WITH audiobooks right here, because at this writing they are the fastest-growing segment of publishing today. I'm likely going to spend more time on audiobooks right here as I might not devote as much in *Book 2: The Book Creation Cycle,* where the focus will likely be print and ebooks.

Should you create an audiobook for your book?

Yes.

When?

Any time, really, but ideally during your beta reader period, which we'll explain in the Book Creation Cycle steps next in Part III of this book and much more deeply in *Book 2: The Book Creation Cycle*. In that period (if you do a beta period) you will be considering fixes, improvements, and suggestions from beta readers in addition to doing other very cool things, but it's also an ideal time to *read your own book aloud* as it *always* turns up at least minor changes and grammatical fixes that might have been missed in editing or not occurred to you previously. When you read out loud you find instances where better diction (choice of words—always opt for simpler, not more decorative or complex, by the way) would make things more clear, and make things flow better for the reader. Your yardstick should be to make sure your reader has an "uninterrupted movie" experience, placing them happily and undistracted in your milieu (sorry, love that word). You might even use your audiobook creation *as* your final proofread. But if not in your beta period, because creating audiobooks takes time, effort, and can take money, any time will do.

On *any* project I recommend an audiobook as well as a hardcover edition. Multiple editions look professional, invite more readers, and hardcovers create higher price points to condition a potential buyer with. Some people can *only* listen to audiobooks, so some will jump on an audio version when they might have balked at a print or ebook, and some will buy your audiobook in addition to your other editions. And a "funnel[46]" arranged with a "bump" (offer to purchase your audiobook while mid-process in signing up for something else) can flip a marketing campaign from a cost to a profit.

But when we talk audiobooks here, we're really not talking about produced CDs with cases. We're talking about digital downloads from sites like Amazon, Audible (which has a subscription service so listeners/readers can enjoy all the audiobooks they can handle), iBooks, KOBO, etc. So, selling and delivering audiobooks, like ebooks, can have an almost-zero cost to produce and deliver. Hence, why indies love audiobooks.

Very much like the KDP and Ingram platforms for ebooks and print books, *ACX* and *Findaway Voices* are the dominant platforms for audiobooks.

ACX[47]

ACX is a subsidiary of Amazon. Follow their recording criteria, which seems to be the more demanding than others, and your files will fly through Findaway Voices (FV). At this writing, ACX has two programs (agreements/contracts):

- Exclusive for seven years with ACX and you get 40%, distributed to Audible, Amazon, and Apple Books.

---

[46] A marketing funnel is a model of the customer journey. It represents the buying stages people go through after becoming aware of a business, service, or product. The funnel shape illustrates the audience narrowing as the journey progresses toward purchase. While you want to minimize dropouts, it's natural for some people to exit at each stage. Your highest-quality leads will make it to the end. —https://www.semrush.com/blog/marketing-funnel

[47] https://www.acx.com/

- Non-exclusive and you get 25%. You can distribute everywhere, including B&N, KOBO, etc.

Do the non-exclusive for the lower, 25 percent royalty. The exclusive deal locks you in for *seven years* (although they say you can opt out with 30-day notice, but I have not tested that). And there is just so much more you can do with your audiobook like direct sales on your website (as a bump!), and you will want it to be published wide with FV, in most cases. Again, Amazon's model seems to strive for *exclusivity* wherever they can get it, and I found it seldom pays, as here with ACX, and as with Kindle Select, save a few exceptions.

ACX does offer coupons you can offer readers.

To upload to ACX, your book will *have to* be already published with KDP, and they will import your metadata and chapter titles into ACX for ease. Your audiobook is then distributed to these retail channels:

- Audible

- Amazon

- Apple Books

FINDAWAY VOICES (FV) [48]

Findaway Voices is how you publish your audiobook *wide,* or to all the other audiobook platforms. I've found FV to be a great platform, easy to use, and you get to select exactly where

---

[48] https://findawayvoices.com/

your audiobook will be distributed ("check box distribution"). Plus, they offer higher royalties (80 percent). Like ACX, they used to (as of this writing they've eliminated it) tempt you with an exclusive agreement, but again, *stay non-exclusive! And be careful to review and select your "program" with any platform, to be clear on the terms!* Interesting, with Findaway Voices (FV) when they had their exclusive option, rather than tempt you with a higher royalty, they offered additional benefits. I don't believe you need them. What you do need is the ability to sell your audiobook in any way and anywhere you want. And FV will also provide coupons you can use in marketing, just as D2D (Draft2Digital) does with ebooks.

And when we say "wide distribution," according to FV, "You have the freedom to set your list price, choose where to sell your audiobook from 40+ partners, and keep 80% of the royalties on every sale.[49]" That includes Audible, Amazon, and Apple Books (formerly iTunes and then iBooks), which you can deselect if you're also publishing with ACX. So, if you have to or prefer to choose just one platform, choose Findaway Voices, because you can publish wide and set your own price.

Here are FV distribution channels, which includes libraries:

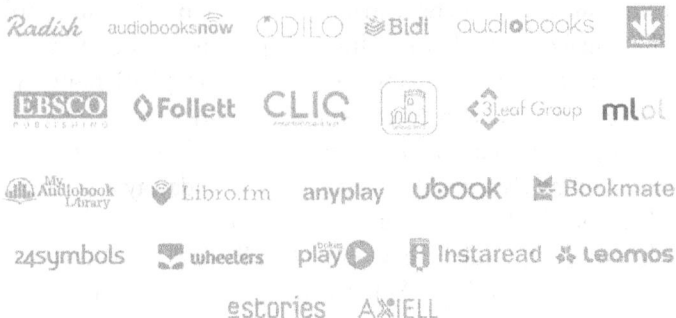

AUDIOBOOK PRODUCTION

To produce your audiobook you will need:

- a separate audio file (MP3) for each chapter

- an audio file for opening credits

- an audio file for closing credits

- a audio file as a "retail audio sample" under five minutes. I use a snippet from somewhere, usually the intro, otherwise apply the writer's principle of *in medias res*[50] and drop your listener right into the

---

[50] In medias res is a literary device that involves starting a story in the middle of a crucial situation that is part of a related chain of events. The situation is an extension of previous events and will be developed in later action. — https://www.britannica.com/art/in-medias-res-literature

action with your sample. Remember, the sample sells the story and the narration.

- You also need files for any other *front and back matter*, such as Acknowledgements and About the Author. (We discuss *parts of a book* in detail and general sequence in the next book, *The Book Creation Cycle.*)

- You'll also need a square version of your book cover.

Once you have properly-produced audio files, both platforms are easy to use. And when your files pass the initial review for proper audio specs upon upload, they then undergo a period of usually ten business days while your quality is checked. That used to be much longer, and has recently changed for the better. *Competition is good.* If there are issues to address you will be notified by email what they are. On my first project I assisted with, my author-client hired a professional recording studio and he narrated his own book, so I was limited to upload of metadata and files, and the files kept coming back with issues. I finally handed the uploads off to his people, and I'm sure they figured out what the issue was (they're pros!), but it taught me to simply make sure all specs are met *before* I upload, and that's easy to do.

When your audiobook passes, your book goes live. As with publishing an eBook to KPD, when you upload your audiobook to ACX and it gets approved after 10 days, it appears for sale almost immediately on Amazon as a new edition of your already-published book in ebook and paperback format. But as with Ingram and their retail channels, your audiobook with Findaway Voices can take some time to appear, as all those retail channels are independent of Findaway Voices (FV).

The hardest part is the production, but even that is fun, actually. I've produced five or six by now[51], and I've enjoyed doing all of them. I've done them from home with the proper equipment and achieved professional results. You can produce your own audiobook, or you can hire a narrator, also called a "producer," as your narrator typically also produces your finished files for you. You can seek and find narrators on either platform, ACX or FV, or you can hire them on Upwork and other places. Some record their audiobooks in professional studios, some record them in a home studio, and some record them in walk-in closets or even in cars—you name it.

If you choose to DIY, invest in a decent microphone. Mine is an $80 Ikedon from Amazon. I love it. I just saw a comparable one in Walmart, of all places, so the availability is big given the popularity of home-studio projects. You'll also need baffling material or a closet, padded room, home studio, and of course, software. It's not really that expensive to get rolling with audiobooks and this might sway you to produce your own from home when compared to studio costs, or perhaps you might even get into the business!

The best advice: Go to YouTube for different home studio setups and equipment recommendations, software explanations (from free to expensive), as well as learning the crafts involved.

The trickiest part is the editing. There are only a few important parameters—noise, volume, before-and-after silence, for example—necessary to get your production sounding full and clean and professional, so your files pass the quality checks by ACX and FV. I subscribe to Adobe Creative Cloud and have access to Adobe Audition, which I love, now that I know how to use it. I learned all I know about producing

---

[51] https://rodneymiles.com/bookstore/

audiobooks from YouTube videos, mostly from Voice Over Angela[52], check her out! But there are free audio programs available that are widely used and produce professional results.

By the way, both ACX and FV have excellent guides on creating audiobooks, and they helped me a lot. That's not always the case—I usually find third-party videos and websites offer product guidance that is better-written, more clear, and more helpful than that shared by the company itself. It seems companies don't try that hard at providing good manuals, maybe because they know third parties will eagerly do it better, but software and other companies usually foster an online *community* where people discuss their use of their products, moderated by someone at the company, and these are usually very helpful.

To plan your audiobook—and what I'm about to share is eerily accurate—take your final word count, divide that by 9,300 to get the approximate hours of listen time your audiobook will be, then multiply that by five to estimate how many hours it will take to create. For example, for a 50,000-word book:

- 50,000 / 9,300 = 5.38 finished audio hours

- 5.38 x 5 = 27 hours of production

- Of those 27 hours, I'd guestimate that we probably have (this is *rough* and varies even in my own projects, but the "27" is reliable)

---

[52] https://www.youtube.com/c/VoiceOverAngela

- o   12 hours of actual recording,

- o   12 hours of editing

- o   3 hours of other stuff—cover creation, uploads, etc.

Remember, with ACX your book has to be live on Amazon before you can create your audiobook, so your metadata is already done and gets imported over to ACX, which makes things pretty easy. You still need a square version of your cover (use 3,000 pixels by 3,000 pixels at 300 dpi), usually, with a "Narrated by ____" added either as a line credit or a badge on your audiobook cover.

Narrators ("producers") usually charge by the *finished audio hour.* So someone charging a more professional rate of $250 per hour will end up costing $1,000 for an audiobook that is a four-hour listen/read. So, if it takes five hours for each finished hour of audio, your narrator/producer is actually making $50 per hour in this case. And that seems to be about the top rate today. You also see narrators willing to work for $100 *per finished audio hour,* which means they are making more like $20 per hour. And what a cool profession to jump into and grow with, if you ask me! If you like the "work," of course.

Any serious author should do this, create an audiobook, even if your book is a "business card," but I'd weigh the time and cost against the hoped-for benefits. It might depend on your target audience. For example, I understand higher-income individuals (probably who use treadmills or have commutes) listen to podcasts more than mere plebians (beach bums like me). So comparing *who* might listen or buy is of course a factor, as well as the simple prestige and having another edition to sell.

ESKIMOS

Now, as we get into *types of books*, as in the qualitative aspects, I'm reminded of a snappy snippet I somehow heard in my younger days in sales, in that colorful world that posited *you can improve yourself* and your *mind determines your reality,* and that world which, now that I think about it, embraced *reading* as a vehicle on that path. That's where books like *Think & Grow Rich* and *How to Win Friends & Influence People,* and where Zig Ziglar's lectures will always hold a special place.

Anyway, the snippet was, "Eskimos have 31 words for *snow.*" I don't know if that's accurate, in fact a quick Brave[53] search suggests at least a few people think there's more than 31, and at least a few think there are fewer, but for our purposes, it matters not. The notion is that a people who are that connected, familiar, and associated with snow would have it understood into distinct types, which is much deeper than us, perhaps, who see all "really cold white stuff that falls from the sky" as simply *snow.*

Well, this is much as the modern author should know their craft, and their specialized terms that serve a purpose. In any profession, the nomenclature is part and parcel of being not just professional but *proficient.* So, when you know what I have observed to be distinct qualitative characteristics of various books, I think it's helpful! It makes setting your goals and how to invest your "beans" (time, scope, resources) so much more clear and easy.

---

[53] https://search.brave.com/

We (indies) are, after all, the proud Eskimos of publishing.

You might decide, "Okay, for now let's get to a *healthy book* ASAP, then a *seasoned book* so we can try for a BookBub deal, and then I don't mind hitting the podcast circuit to eventually have a *phenomenon* on my hands, but before any of that, we want at least a *good book.* What do each involve?" You can then string a line from here to there, your *good* or even a *great* book.

What is a *successful* book? For most it means sales, reviews, and rank. This is probably as far as most people think on the subject, and I'm not sure they even know what *they* think "success" means, if asked, other than that. Some authors don't really care about sales, they care about *being an author* as part of their effort to raise rates, engage with prospects, coach their clients, get on stage, podcasts, or radio or TV. Or their first book was *soft launched* as part of a larger picture to get to three, five, or seven books and *then* promote and voila, they're a financially viable author who has *new choices in life.*

I had a prospect late for our meeting ask, "What's your most successful book?" without a smile. I've had books sell thousands of copies, launch new careers, fulfil personal dreams, delight a child, so I guess it's hard to say. I knew what he meant, and decided if that was his only criteria (he had an assistant licking his boots the whole way), working with him was going to be a humorless, lifeless experience, the kind I've worked so hard to *not* be a part of, and I withdrew my offer to work with them.

Who you choose not to work with is every bit as important as who you choose to work with. My most precious commodity is time, in addition to where and with whom I apply what talent, skill, and passion I have, and when you start compromising on your terms, you have started your exit from that field, and I don't plan to leave it that way. Besides, there are, what, eight billion people on Earth? Scarcity mindsets lead to regrets. It's only in an abundance mindset do we see clearly where we want to go and sense any kind of ease to getting there. Letting go of good to get to great pays, not just in the long run, and it feels... great.

When you boil it down, each of us who creates a *good* book has succeeded. Big time. But what is a *good* book?

That starts with understanding *expectations*.

EXPECTATIONS

The subject of *expectations* is important for us right about now. A great *negative* example is found with a podcast I listened to on the subject of publishing, which included really great authors, great interviews, and great insights, but when they published their own book I was shocked. The cover had the appearance of a young adult fiction novel. Probably a comedy. But I knew it was on the subject of publishing. They violated the *expectation* for their own genre.

Now, it's very true that authors sometimes reinvent or violate these "rules" or expectations, and no worries. Cormac McCarthy, adored in the halls of enduring literature, uses scant punctuation—well, no quotation marks, anyway. But he does it in such a consistent way it *works*. So, I'm not trying to make you sell out your craft or your mind or heart, I'm trying to help you, if not to sell your book, at least get it properly identified by readers.

Formulas, expectations, tropes[54], all actually have a place, no matter what or how you write. Movies and books follow a

---

[54] trope (noun) \ ˈtrōp \ 1a: a word or expression used in a figurative sense : FIGURE OF SPEECH; b: a common or overused theme or device : CLICHÉ (the usual horror movie tropes); borrowed from Greek -tropos "turned, directed, living (in the manner indicated)," adjective derivative of trópos "turn, way, manner, style" —https://www.merriam-webster.com/dictionary/trope

formula (like the *hero's journey*[55]) because they *imitate life.* When I design a book cover there are certain important considerations and differences by genre. See Derek Murphy, the cover design master. He's the dude who hosts the writing retreats in castles, by the way.[56]

Critical components of a professional book cover include:

- Design expectations for your genre

- A provocative title and cover image (if used)

- A subtitle that accurately sets expectations

- Color contrast

- Professional appearance.

That last item is the career-developer. *What makes one cover look professional when another doesn't?* There are lots of answers, like clean design, images that work together, uncommon fonts (and not more than use of *two* fonts, ideally one serif and one sans-serif), good use of *semiotics*—instant communication through imagery, colors, etc.

And again, genre *expectations.*

---

[55] Hands up if you've heard this story before: A lonely hero who is trying to find himself. A sudden and unexpected journey, promising adventure and peril. A test of character, strength, and skill. An ultimate battle that tests the hero's resolve. A triumphant return home... If this sounds familiar, that's because this exact narrative template has inspired countless stories from ancient myths to modern television shows and movies. This template is known as the "monomyth"—or, colloquially, the hero's journey. —https://www.masterclass.com/articles/writing-101-what-is-the-heros-journey

[56] https://www.creativindiecovers.com/author/admin/

You can answer most of these questions for yourself, *but you have to ask yourself these questions.* And the best place to do this kind of exercise is in a bookstore, ideally a big one like Barnes & Noble. It can be done viewing books on Amazon, but it's not nearly as effective or fun as being in a bookstore. Pick up books in your genre and feel them, study them. What do like about them? What makes them look professional?

Interestingly, *good reviews* are more a matter of *accurate expectations* than a quality book. I know, right? Check that out—Read some reviews of books on Amazon and see what the bad reviews complain about. Many gripe about their *expectations* not being met. It's actually *truth in advertising*, if you think about it. In fact, reading reviews to see what readers *want* is a powerful idea I got from Chris Fox[57]. And in *Book 2* we look at actual one-star reviews!

On expectations, on being *identifiable* and on design, I learned from a chess analogy I was once given. A friend taught chess to high school students and we were talking about chess.

"I want to get a board with Revolutionary War pieces," I said, brightly.

"No, you don't." he said.

"Why not?"

"The pieces are hard to recognize. You'll spend half your time in your head confirming what each piece is. The best chess sets have the same old, regular-shaped pieces so they are easy to recognize."

Brilliant!

Remember, the whole point of design and organization, diction, grammar, flow, tone, consistent spelling, is to get your message across, as cleanly and clearly, with as much assimilation or enjoyment on the reader's end as possible.

---

[57] https://www.chrisfoxwrites.com/write-faster-write-smarter/

That's it. We're not getting a grade in high school English. We're teaching your rights as a living person, or whisking you away to a fantasy land as an escape and stimulation of your mind, we're sharing expertise to help people, we're seeking a tribe we might engage with, sometimes for the culture, sometimes for profit, sometimes both. That's what matters.

A coffee table book is by definition not in a 5" x 8" *trim size* (book height and width), nor is a romance novel in 8.5" by 8.5" hardcover. So even trim size is a matter of genre and expectation.

Existing *expectations* by genre should be known by the modern author, so you can meet, and if possible, exceed them.

BOOKS THAT SUCK

We are about to conceive, plan, and launch your book project, so what makes for good and bad book experiences? One of very few "bad" book experiences I've had was with a James Patterson novel. Understand, Patterson didn't write the book I'm speaking of, I'm sure. Patterson is a *franchise.* He apparently hires authors to write formulaic novels and stamps his recognizable name (brand) on them. In fairness, they are in the main admittedly escapist "beach reads," and in fairness, I've only read one full novel of "his," but I learned a lot.

I met a girl reading while working at a community center who stated she hated James Patterson, which struck me as odd—*How, why, would you "hate" any author?* So I went to a grocery store and bought a "summer read" by Patterson and another author who shall remain nameless. All chapters were one-to-three-pages long, which got annoying quickly, but suggested the target reader had a tiny attention span or read on breaks, I guess. (I do believe in dividing things up for comfort, for having lots of milestones and a sense you are progressing, and again it depends on expectations by genre.)

But then the end of this "novel" was nothing more than a call to action for the next book—no real resolution of the two-dimensional characters or cheesy, cliché plot. Just glitzy locations and a dash of predictable intrigue, *and I hated James Patterson, too.* I actually felt ripped off, something I've never really experienced with a book before that.

The amazing irony is, and in fairness to Patterson, it was he, in a Master Class I'd been gifted, who stated reading a book gives a sense of *accomplishment.* I'd never considered that before, but it does, doesn't it? (An advance review I've gotten on this book stated he felt like he'd accomplished something!) More than that is the expected *satisfaction* books are expected to deliver. It—satisfaction—is part of what makes a book (and author) *good.*

But books that don't deliver *suck.*

If a book is losing you, you need to focus more and enjoy your read or you need to put that book down and move on to another one. Lots of fish in the sea. Unless you're obligated in some way to grind through a text, protect your love of reading, for God's sake.

Different books have different purposes and expectations:

- Non-fiction: Solve a problem, inform, advise, remember, etc.

- Fiction: Escape, imagine, consider, dream, etc.

Failing the reader's purpose creates a book that *sucks.* Other things can make a book suck, and sometimes destroy your credibility as an author, such as:

- Lack of editing

- Amateur book cover and interior (under-done or over-done) design

- Small size (word count). For example, if a romance novel is under 30,000 words the reviewers will complain!

- Ebook format only

- Setting wrong expectations in your cover, title, subtitle

- Lack of personal story/engagement

- Obvious "book as a sales pitch" for other services

- *And so many more…*

Books that suck fail to meet expectations, stated or implied, and that includes being useful and being satisfying. Or it can just be that even with great info or story they are ugly or carelessly presented in some way.

GOOD BOOKS

"Good" books meet or exceed expectations. They make you *think*. They satisfy or solve a problem. They accomplish what you as a reader had hoped for. For this very basic reason I have encouraged experts publishing "business card" books to not fall into the trap of "giving just enough info to screw someone up enough they seek you out." There's no need. An author-turned speaker once explained, "Put it all out there, put it all in your book and people will still pay you to say it live." And I recall Robert Heinlein in a *great book* (we'll define these in a moment) on writing science fiction, explaining he was willing to share all of his secrets because hardly anyone would actually apply them. So, put it all out there. They will still come to you, even if a few run with your ideas and don't need you further, and isn't that okay as well?

In fact, when I started to succeed in another life as a real estate agent under a successful broker's tutelage, I asked her, "Why am I doing so well with your advice, when all these other agents have been given the same advice?"

Without hesitation she told me, "You're the only one who has done what I told you to do."

So a *good book* delivers, maybe even fearlessly.

What else makes a good book?

Well, how do *you* recognize a good book?

In addition to *delivering,* another definition of *good book* for a popular audience is simply one that flows so well your reader thinks they're having fun, wants to find out more, and turns pages—it's a *page-turner.* They enjoy a story or get information effortlessly. It's clear. It doesn't have distractions like bad grammar or spelling or design—anything that detracts from the message or story. It has enough in it to satisfy the expectations it itself has set through description and design. It is designed and formatted professionally. There are even some you might like to read again, from time-to-time.

In fact, I've learned a *brand,* for that matter, is a *promise.* In her brilliant book on the subject, branding expert and author Lauren Clemett explains:

> "You need to ensure your brand speaks to the perceived and the real value it delivers. This is called the *brand promise*."
>
> —LAUREN CLEMETT,
> Author of *Your Brand True North*[58]

Your book is a part of your author brand, of course. And while you certainly can be brilliant, completely different, or pen enduring literature, none of that is required for wild success. But you do have to deliver on what promises are made, and those promises are made, initially, in your *basics:*

- Cover design

- Subtitle

- Blurb

You then follow up with your content and the value you provide *inside* the book. If they match, that's a *good book*. If we look at what's promised in the packaging and find what's inside doesn't really match, well... time for more development of your content or your packaging or both. It also maps a path, if we reverse engineer your book. For example, I usually don't commit to providing cover design ideas until I've gotten knee-deep into a draft and if applicable, consulted the author-client's brand, usually by way of website, at least by discussing goals. Sometimes I'm provided a *brand guide* by the author's

---

[58] https://yourbrandtruenorth.com/finding-your-brand-true-north-book/

branding or marketing person, which can include colors, logos, images, and so on.

This also explains why we generally write both your Introduction and Conclusion *last*.

Consistency is king.

Beyond that, good books can vary from reader-to-reader, audience-to-audience. If you really care, do as Chris Fox advises and read the reviews of books in your genre to see what readers want, expect, and what makes them bitch or celebrate.

One time when my daughter was little, we were setting the house up for her birthday party. As I was finishing cleaning up the guest bathroom, I told her, "Fallon, go get a really nice bath towel." I had a few in mind. She came back with a beach towel with a howling wolf printed on it. I laughed, paused, looked at it, and realized, *This is a really nice towel to her, and probably to her 12-year-old guests as well.* So, we went with it! And I learned something right there. It was nice. I felt good about it.

We all have our faves. Mine used to be science fiction, then business, then biography, then narrative non-fiction, always philosophy—shit, I love them all, I think.

What are yours?

Why? What do they offer and what do they give?

My favorite way in the world to choose a book is in a bookstore with a big selection, where I can take a few on what I'm looking for, go sit with them, rule a few out, and pick one that resonates. The same subject can be approached from different ways, even if they are all *good books*. In this way I've found a few *great books*. And if I can't get to a Barnes & Noble a decent library will do (although a large bookstore is better), and if I can't get to a library I can read multiple book pages on Amazon.

Of course, both *good* and *great* books are generally well-written, professionally edited, helpful or profound or entertaining, and usually nicely packaged (although classic books often no longer need the packaging).

A *good book* or even a *great book* can also get its strength from a single, powerful *idea* (such as *Start with Why* by Simon Sinek, or *Built to Last* by Jim Collins, or *Ender's Game* by Orson Scott Card, or…) along with being well-written. And "well-written" can be "written shitty then edited."

This all applies when you plan your book, and definitely as you write, certainly when you have your first/rough/ugly draft, again when you have your *beta copies* out there with *beta readers,* and of course, when published.

The test?

Look over and read your own book not as a writer, but *as a reader.*

Great Books

So, what makes a book *great?* For one thing, great books make you *think and feel.* They exceed expectations. They earn a place in your memory—a good place. One way make a good book great is add a *great ending.* As a science fiction writer, L. Ron Hubbard's *Battlefield Earth* is a good book with a great ending. Interesting, a clerk at Waldenbooks in another time and place, seeing I was buying Stephen R. Donaldson's *The Real Story,* pointed out she was not going to buy Donaldson's series until she knew he finished it. Never occurred to me! I bought it anyway, and he did finish the series (*phew*). And at the time, it was *great,* just like his previous series, *The Chronicles of Thomas Covenant the Unbeliever,* which was great because at times it was *riveting.* I'd walk across campus at

University of Florida and *read it,* it was so good. Near the end, I remember making time to finish it in my apartment (in the "student ghetto"), and *pacing around the room* as I finished it.

Great book series.

But as we talked books, on Hubbard she commented, "He cares more about his ideas than his characters." True enough. But *Battlefield Earth* is fun, is a good 1,000-page book, and the end is great, if you ask me. I won't spoil it, but maybe it informs one way we make a book *great.* The end is set down the road from the timeline of the story itself, epilogue-ish, and with one simple act, the ending sets the main story on a shelf as a sort of legend, and the simple physical act at the end made it both *memorable and nostalgic,* at least for me.

Which leads me to Hemingway, and why I love his work. Hemingway wrote in large from his memory, with great attention on details or "periphery" in his "Iceberg Theory," presenting just enough to trigger thoughts and feelings in his reader's minds. He'd edit a draft down to the *only-necessary* parts. I understand he'd take a 150,000-word draft and edit it down to more like 50,000 words. When I was taught creative writing in college in the late 1980s, it was Hemingway and the *modern novel* they were teaching. "Write about periphery," in books, poems. Hemingway's stated goal was to write in such a realistic way that the events in his books became more like actual memories in readers' minds than fiction.

And it worked. There are parts in *The Sun Also Rises* that hit me in the gut, and he does it with what is *not* stated, especially the scene where Jake returns to the café to find Lady Ashley *gone.* It's a kick in the balls.

> *Great books make you feel… usually awakened*
> *or inspired, or sometimes simply a bit of the*
> *pain we all feel from time-to-time.*

137

"I've learned that people will forget what
you said, people will forget what you did,
but people will never forget how you made
them feel."

— MAYA ANGELOU

And, like paintings and poems or anything for that matter, when books are professionally done, well-thought and written, they are practically "good" on those bases alone, even before we get to the *idea* of the book. *Technical expertise is part of good and great art.* But when we start talking about the book's *idea,* that seems to be where most *great* books are born. It's often the *idea* that makes a book *important* or *timely* or *timeless and universal,* and that can make a book *great.*

When I used to read *MAD Magazine* as a kid, it was always exciting and challenging and new, because some of it was very visual and obvious and some of it I had to figure out at that young age. It was *great.* Later, in my twenties, I used to read a lot of *Calvin and Hobbes* and it was *great* because it always made me *feel* good.

But books do that, don't they?

Good satisfies or solves a problem, or takes your mind off of other things (healthy escapism) and makes you think. *Great* books make you feel—excitement, empathy, wonder, fear, hate—whatever you dig feeling, and great *inspires.* And when we *feel* we know we're *alive.* Reading can do that.

What books have *you* found *great*? I don't mean what books have you read that have been described "as great" by others, but which have *you* found great? Why? The characters? The stories? The insights or the wisdom? The entertainment or the ideas of the future? Did it help you, propel you to new places or get you back on your natural track? Did it make you *feel?*

We get to do that, as authors.

In fact, it's *artists who create visions of what might be.* Like science fiction—it serves a very important purpose, actually.

Creating a *great* book doesn't mean you have to do something not done before or change the rules of grammar or have sparks fly out of the pages when people open it. I think taking a book from good to great requires flexibility, input, editing, and *passion or love.* How an author feels about their subject usually comes through the read and is called the *tone.* Build upon a balance of technical expertise (yours or hired) and *passion.* And it comes through if the writing and the voice aren't cluttered by mistakes or inconsistencies.

A *great book* can also be as simple as handily triggering a reader's *imagination.* This is actually one of the aspects that sets books apart from other media, and why perhaps, people really love science fiction and fantasy. You feel like you've spent time in another, often magical world, where all ends well, people find redemption, restoration, learn, transform, save the world, or at least go about a hero's journey.

The good news is we don't all need to write *great* books, as fun as it is to try. We do need to write *good books,* however. We need to avoid writing *derivative* books (see below), and work to write *transformative books* and ensure we have *healthy* and *successful* books, and when needed, a *seasoned book* (again, see below), which is not a matter of chance at all, not anymore. It's hard science today.

With the steps and processes in this book series you can produce *good, transformative, healthy, successful* books with confidence. And you can produce them more quickly and reliably. You can publish and market with your eyes open. And if you can do that, you can become a full-time author, if that's what you want. The variable is time, effort, and the demand for your subject matter. Or, you can produce books you and others will love or appreciate part-time, as a passion or in support of a (sometimes new) profession. It's up to you.

When you yourself have views on what makes a book *good or great,* you are more capable and more likely to produce one. First—always first—*create your book for you.* Clint Eastwood said he didn't know if anyone would like his films, but he knew *he* would. So that's the place to start, of course. Your book *will* outlive you, and you deserve to live happily with it the rest of your life.

Heck, you might even write more if you do.

ORIGINAL BOOKS

People often worry about their content being original or taking from another's work, so this is a good time to address this. First, you can check your content with a website called Copyscape[59]. There, you upload text to have it checked against existing uses on the Internet. You can check your content for originality by simply pasting a snippet of writing in the search bar and see what comes up. Many freelance clients in the know require a "Copyscape pass" to know they are clear to use the provided language. I recently copy edited a book for a client and searched a phrase to find they had pretty much quoted the bulk of an article word-for-word. *Ugh.* I rewrote the language to clear it, and my worry was allayed only when I

---

[59] https://www.copyscape.com/

stepped back and realized the whole work was *transformative*, and we were indeed giving credit where it was needed.

FAIR USE

First, how much of another's work can you quote in your own book? I've looked into this through the years and heard all kinds of ideas, such as "ten percent of the original work" or "28 words" or "short passages" or "anything considered *fair use*," or "just don't get caught." I resolved, given the ambiguity around the issue, that probably the worst that can happen is to get some kind of notice or maybe even a cease and desist order, at which point you might remove the passage and re-publish. Easy nowadays. And there's a difference between law and enforcement, but what's "okay," anyway, ethically? *What would I be okay with as far as others quoting me?*

To that, *quote me all you like!* Just don't try to pass my ideas or too many of my exact words off as your own *for your own gain.*

In general it's simple enough to just use short passages and give credit where credit is due. Celebrities decided in their pursuit of attention they no longer need a presumption of privacy, in many ways. And *referring to something, quoting something and providing credit is not plagiarism.* That didn't stop Disney from filing a very ugly lawsuit against a small daycare for painting a pseudo Mickey Mouse® on the exterior wall where the kids played.

But I really like this answer from DoctorOddFellow on Reddit from six years ago[60], so now I'm going to use another's

---

[60]

https://www.reddit.com/r/writing/comments/6m5eoa/how_much_of_a_book_can_you_legally_quote/

material in explaining how much of another's material we can generally use:

> "If you don't get permission, then the answer is 'as much as you can without pissing off the copyright owner and getting yourself sued.' … In other words, there is no hard and fast rule here. In the U.S., using someone else's work without permission is infringement, but the copyright law also provides for the concept of *fair use*… Only a court can determine whether an infringement (using someone's work without permission) can be considered an exception under the fair use doctrine… When the court is making that determination they look at … 'the amount and substantiality of the portion used in relation to the copyrighted work as a whole…'
>
> "A few lines properly cited? No problem; a copyright owner would be hard-pressed to make a case out of that. One to three paragraphs quoted and properly cited -- almost certainly still safe. A full page? Now it starts to get dicey. A full page out of *War and Peace* may not be an issue, but a full page quoted out of a 12-page article may cause a court to decide that the 'substantiality of the portion used in relation to the copyrighted work as a whole' means it's not fair use. A whole chapter? Yeah, that's almost certainly not fair use."

Here's another really good article for your spare time: https://stevelaube.com/how-much-can-i-quote-from-another-source-without-permission/.

I think that's all good guidance and important, but the real question is whether a work is *transformative* or simply *derivative*.

TRANSFORMATIVE VS. DERIVATIVE

It's even more important to understand the difference between *transformative* and *derivative* works. You want your book to be transformative, and not derivative. Early on as a ghostwriter, mainly of web-researched short books of expertise, I had to figure out what material created by others was okay and not okay to use, and how to give proper credit, create acceptable citations, and so on.

So, at the 30,000-foot level, I came to understand what seems like a healthy approach as reflected in law. I'm not a lawyer, but there is a lot of guidance available and we should *all* have more of a grip on the law *for ourselves*.

Interesting, back then experts paid me to research and write *their* books of expertise in many cases, in one case for a college professor. Today I no longer "ghostwrite," but I'm still thrilled when in working a project the author-client-expert evolves their own procedure or terminology. I often get to be a sounding board for that and it's cool.

Also interesting, regarding all kinds of popular books—fiction, celebrity cookbooks, and so on, it's estimated around 70 percent of the best sellers on the racks at your grocery store are *ghostwritten*. But I digress...

It's *not okay* to take someone else's work and call it your own (derivative). What is okay is to take another's work and either apply it more specifically or more broadly or in a new way (transformative). I believe the law sees it this way because *derivative* works take from the Great Library, and *transformative* works add to it. Think about it.

We'll look at a few definitions and you'll get it, and it's important to understand. Clients ask all the time about this, in fact it's a little worrisome when they don't! And it's easy once you understand what follows here. You can proceed without worry, actually, if you apply this to your own book. Look at the sources of these quotes. (The NOLO site is a great resource for DIY legal, by the way.)

> "… 'transformative' uses are more likely to be considered fair. Transformative uses are those that add something new, with a further purpose or different character, and do not substitute for the original use of the work."
>
> —https://www.copyright.gov/fair-use/

> "A derivative work is a work based on or derived from one or more already existing works. Common derivative works include translations, musical arrangements, motion picture versions of literary material or plays, art reproductions, abridgments, and condensations of preexisting works."
>
> —https://www.copyright.gov/circs/circ14.pdf

> "Copyright law gives authors certain exclusive rights to their work. These rights

include the exclusive right to reproduce or resell the work. However, the fair use doctrine, codified in federal law as 17 U.S. Code § 107, is a defense that allows an 'infringer' to make limited use of the original author's work without asking permission. Without the fair use doctrine, this would qualify as copyright infringement.

"Courts will consider four primary factors in determining whether a particular use qualifies as 'fair.' One of the factors weighing in favor of finding fair use is when the use of the original material is 'transformative.' Transformative uses take the original copyrighted work and transform its appearance or nature to such a high degree that the use no longer qualifies as infringing."

—https://www.nolo.com/legal-encyclopedia/fair-use-what-transformative.html

Once I understood this and how the law sees this, I felt unchained in my writing. It made sense to me that as a culture we reward progress for the greater good and we punish stealing. Simple.

By the way, "copyright" applies to written works and music. In the U.S., your copy*right* is automatic once you publish your work. So, for about a decade I never recommended registering your copyright. Why pay the fee? Then I had a little scare with ACX (Amazon audiobooks platform). As I started my audiobook project ACX Support told me someone had already claimed the rights to my book. I really thought I was about to have a copyright battle on my hands. I made a case with Support, sending a screenshot of the copyright page as it appeared on Amazon (in the Look Inside feature) with my name as the copyright holder, but as I waited on the response my policy on registering copyrights changed! In a few days Support got back and let me know all was well, thanks for clearing it up. *A human, intelligent response!* But I came to see copyright as we're taught about contracts in real estate school: Verbal contracts are *legal* but only written contracts are *enforceable.* The point? Always register your copyright. It's only $65 in the U.S. and can save a big headache in the future.

By the way, if you have a particular term or brand name, you might want to register a *trademark,* and if you have a design or invention, you'll want to register a *patent.*

And be careful! I found out by accident early on when two authors who co-wrote a book using my services later on broke up and then each tried to publish the same book, that *I had rights as the creator of the work.* Amazon's stance was, "You two figure it out. Meanwhile, we're taking it down," (paraphrase). It's actually a built-in protection for ghostwriters and collaborators, but important for you to know, obviously. Since then I always note on my invoices, "All rights convey with full payment of all invoices," which, with a paid receipt, my clients can always use if they need to, or I am happy to sign a release.

Understanding the purpose here is the important thing— The society *needs and wants* improvement, new uses, progress, but should not tolerate stealing or assuming credit where it is not due.

HEALTHY BOOKS

I started using the term "healthy book" somewhere along the way, and it simply means that once published, like a baby who has made it through that first year or two and can now walk and start to take care of themselves a little bit, even minimally, a healthy book:

- Is well written and professionally edited (that can be done by you, but ideally by someone else carefully chosen).

- Has a professional-looking cover appropriate for its genre and audience.

- Has good *marketing copy* (not hard, formula for this to follow in *Book 2*), otherwise known as a "book marketing description" or "blurb."

- Is available for purchase.

- Has at least 15 reviews on Amazon. (Or, the dominant platform of your day. Amazon only considers a product "retail ready" when it has at least 15 reviews.)

- Delivers what it promises.

That book stands a fighting chance. The baby analogy is a good one. I asked my mother (I'm 53 at this writing) one day, as I had a child of my own who was nearing adulthood and learning to drive, "Mom, do we if we ever stop worrying about our kids?"

"No," she said, "we just get used to it." And she smiled.

Maybe it's not as dramatic with books. But once you have the basics in, it does get easier. A book with 200 reviews will be easier to sell than one with 2, obviously. To boot, Amazon will be more interested in selling it for you—and they might not care at all until you have 15 ratings and reviews, which is what Amazon calls "retail ready," or a *healthy* book in Amazon's eyes.

You can promote a book more effectively and better use it as leverage for other things once it's *healthy.*

And the beauty of self/digital publishing is you can always tweak. Some authors substitute one of their seven keywords in the KDP metadata and see what happens to their sales. If they go up, they leave it and test another new one. If it drops, they replace the old one. But once rolling, there are myriad ways to tweak and improve performance. That's how granular you can get with this, and many do. How great though, if that's your "job," right?

And a book can become a best seller at any time, you're not limited to your launch.

Seasoned Books (& BookBub)

I realized a new term would be useful—and the idea behind all of these book designations is *usefulness,* by the way—to describe what you need to qualify for certain promotional campaigns such as BookBub. In order to be *eligible* for a BookBub Featured Deal, before they will even consider your book, it needs to meet certain criteria and I've based my description of a *seasoned book* largely around BookBub Featured Deal minimum requirements and submission tips[61]. See, this is clearly how BookBub has established such a strong presence as the leader in what are called "promo sites," email subscriptions that deliver daily or weekly emails letting you in on deals, usually on ebooks, and regarded as some of the most effective promotions by authors:

- **A retail price established over time**, high enough that it can be offered at least 50 percent off for the promotion, if not for free. And it can't be offered for a lower/better price in the last 30 days (used to be 60). If we're gearing up to apply for a BookBub Featured Deal, we will set our retail price in what I call *market range* for at least 30 days prior to applying and offering your book at a discount.

- Content that is **error-free**—well-formatted and free of typos and grammatical errors.

- "A **full-length book**. Novels and collections of short stories or novellas should be at least 150 pages in length, works of nonfiction at least 100 pages, cookbooks at least 70 pages, middle grade books at least 100 pages, and children's picture books at least

---

[61] https://www.bookbub.com/partners/featured_deals

20 pages." (No stand-alone novellas or short stories.)[62]

- **"Available on at least one of our supported retailers**. We only feature deals that are available on Amazon, Kobo, Barnes and Noble, Google Play, or Apple Books in the US, UK, Canada, or Australia."[63]

Add to this that BookBub will not feature the same book more than once every six months nor feature the same author more than once every 30 days, and even if you meet all of these requirements, it does not guarantee you will have the privilege of paying a significant fee to have your discounted book featured! In fact if you submit and are rejected, you have to wait "at least four weeks before" re-applying.

Yet, or maybe because of this stringent (but very do-able) criteria, BookBub is one of the most reliable forms of promotion according to many authors. Realize, if your campaign at least breaks even it might be a success in terms of new readers. More reason to publish multiple books in series or at least in the same genre or subject, and to consider funnels and bumps for cash flow.

At this writing, BookBub also offers a weekly "New Releases for Less," which you can submit for consideration at any time within six months *prior to* your release date. Your

---

[62] While most clients talk in terms of *pages,* most writers talk in terms of *word count.* I have often calculated word count by taking pages and multiplying by what I estimate the words per page to be (how many words across, usually 12, by number of lines, often 35 or so). As a writer, *words* tells me much more, as pages can vary wildly depending on current trim/page size, fonts, interior design, if there are images, and so on. And with word count, there are expectations by genre (of course). We'll talk more about this also in *Book 2: The Book Creation Cycle.*

[63] https://www.bookbub.com/partners/featured_deals

book does *not* have to be discounted (but priced reasonably) but again, BookBub promotions are hard to land. I've had a celebrity's book get turned down, so they're very picky about what books they offer a "deal" on. If yours does get accepted by BookBub, expect to pay $2,000 to $4,000 for a full deal, but your book will be seen by *millions of targeted readers*. To help get your book "accepted," have all your basics in and also have advance *editorial reviews* from bloggers, readers, and other authors. This we usually accomplish in our *beta period,* but more on that in *Book 2: The Book Creation Cycle,* and *Book 3: Exponential Author Growth.*

I'd add to "seasoned book" that it has to have at least 25 customer reviews. In fact, if we look further at BookBub's "submission tips[64]" they include:

- "Accumulate reader reviews."

- "Have a professionally designed cover optimized for your genre."

- "Garner critical reviews." (These are not customer but editorial and other reviews.)

- "Optimize your retailer product page description."

- "Discount your book on all retailers."

In fact, the article is so excellent, here's that link again: https://insights.bookbub.com/tips-on-optimizing-your-

---

[64] https://insights.bookbub.com/tips-on-optimizing-your-submission-for-a-bookbub-featured-deal/

submission-for-a-bookbub-featured-deal/, because they are *all extremely useful tips, whether you are in this primarily for book sales or author altitude.*

Taken from my real estate days, when we'd discuss a *refinance,* it was always said the original loan had to be "seasoned." It means the loan (or book) is to some degree proven. It's been around the block. So, a "seasoned" book is one that meets at least a minimum criteria and becomes very useful for those authors whether seeking sales, credibility, or opportunities to be taken seriously and promoted among other seasoned books.

SUCCESSFUL BOOKS

Penultimately[65], and maybe most relevant for the journey we are about to take in planning and creating our book, "What is a *successful* book?" It is, of course, a "book that sells a lot," but for the modern author that's a limited view.

A successful book meets or exceeds the goals stated at the outset of your book project.

Common goals include:

- Book sales.

- Becoming a full-time author.

---

[65] "Next to last." I hate to drop a big word like this but it seems to come up in publishing, and you're now a modern author, so…

- Increased credibility for higher rates or to launch a speaking or coaching or consulting career.

- Memorialization of your life and times—a legacy and/or family info.

- Awareness and the spread of a message or cause.

- Scaling any information or activity by making access easy, cheap, and global.

- Any combination of the above or more.

The first thing I like to do with any client and for my own publishing is think about and discuss and clarify *why* I'm writing the book and what I hope to get out of it, as well as what I hope for my readers. Many dive in without clarifying these things, but many also aren't aware of some of the possibilities. Or they might have false or misguided hopes. So it's a worthy discussion and a perfect start to a project.

Some examples of likely goals by genre:

- **Memoir**: Primarily to tell your story for the benefit and entertainment of others, often family or people going through what you've been through. Often to make money as well.

- **Book of expertise**: To share your expertise for the benefit of others who might need it, often to establish yourself as an expert in that area and take a local practice national, make the jump into public speaking and/or coaching and consulting, and to be able to command higher rates. Just the simple fact of publishing a book generally establishes you as an expert.

- **Fiction, historical fiction, narrative non-fiction**: To entertain and enlighten based on your imagination, ideas, and/or research. To build a readership to where you have thousands waiting to buy your next book, thereby becoming a viable, full-time author.

Other goals include:

- Have a "hub" for your branding and marketing.

- Email list growth.

- Your book successfully funneling people onto other services.

- Use your book as the framework for a course (turning your Table of Contents "on its side").

Whatever it is, shake it out at the start because this is part of the fun *and your goal(s) affect every part of your book project.* We get these real-life results all the time. Goals should be realistic, and you might not know what "realistic publishing goals" are without the input of a consultant.

What does success mean for you, with your book?

The benefits might not even be known or expected. My client and friend and incredible woman Erin Mahoney[66] who invented the Girl Power Go[67] program was initially turned away by American Girl, but after her books (guidebook and journal) came out *they approached her* and offered her a contract for dual promotions. One of my first full-book projects, another amazing woman, Cynthia Freeman[68] knew she wanted to memorialize and preserve her vast coaching expertise. (She was with Tony Robbins[69] before he was mega-author, coach, and speaker "Tony Robbins.") What she didn't expect was how clients would enjoy the addition of the book to her coaching. For example, she started instructing them, "Go to page such-and-such" as an aid to their work together. Her excellent book, *The Power of Done,* became a new tool to coach with. Very cool.

There are many ways your book can be a successful one.

In a podcast, guest Joanne Harris[70] (author of *Chocolat* and so many novels in multiple genres) said no one prepared her for success. Lots of people prepared her for failure, but no one prepared her for success. Well, I'd like to prepare you for success as much as possible, and it starts with simply… defining success. With success defined, does your book do *that?* Then it is a successful book.

PHENOMENAL BOOKS

When starting out on a project it's a great idea to find "comparable books." In real estate we'd "run comps" to arrive at a probable selling price for a home, and books are no different. With *comparable books* you learn so much about what's "hot" or "successful" in your genre *right now.* You learn what's contemporary about design, expectations, how the blurbs are written, what readers want, like or complain about, and you can then deduce a *market range* for pricing.

On a recent project I was looking over several *successful, seasoned* books on private equity, and *$100M Offers* by Alex Hormozi came up, and *wow.* I always look at reviews as a byproduct of both how people like a book and how it's selling, and Hormozi's (at this writing) had over 16,000 customer reviews on Amazon. *That gets my attention! Phenomenal!*

First, a primer on Amazon customer reviews, since we're using that as one indicator of a book's success:

REVIEWS IN A GLANCE

- A "ghost town" book has no reviews.

- A "family and friends" book might have up to 10 customer reviews on Amazon.

- A "retail-ready" book has 15 or more.

- A "seasoned" book has 25 or more.

- When a book approaches and exceeds 100 reviews I really believe the Amazon algorithm warms up to it. Amazon makes money when *you* make sales, but they have to decide—with an algorithm—which books to put their attention on and promote.

- Books with *hundreds* of reviews are very likely very "successful" for their authors.

- Books with *thousands* of reviews are usually national or international bona fide *best sellers,* the old-school kind, and/or have a celebrity's name on them. Either way, or maybe especially if the author is not a household name, a book with thousands of positive reviews is a *phenomenon.*

Again, Alex Hormozi's book, at this writing, has over 16,000 positive customer reviews. It makes me sit up and pay attention: *What did he do to do that? What is the book about? Is it really that good? What does he do? And who the hell is he, anyway?*

Phenomenal books simply stand out in some pronounced way, and perhaps we all dream of having one. Not sure I do— I just want to make a happy life writing and publishing them. A *good* and a *great book* here and there will do it! But *phenomenal books* do happen, just as "lightning strikes" do, in a marketing sense—the overnight success, and so on.

We could add to *phenomenal books,* of course, those that are "more than great." Certainly *Don Quixote* (1605), by Miguel de Cervantes, which Thomas Jefferson liked so much he had several editions in different languages on his shelves at his home in Monticello, last I visited there. Of course, *The Bible,* and any others that seem staples in a genre or field, like

The Chicago Manual of Style or the much shorter *Elements of Style* by Strunk and White. You know what I'm talking about, I'm sure. Books you feel you'd not only read again but feel you have to have on your shelves. Staples in your library.

Which for you spring to mind? What makes them *phenomenal?*

———

We *modern authors* know what the possibilities are. Let's look at a few more important terms, and then, last at, *how* you make your book *healthy, successful, and even great.*

MODERN MEANINGS:
IS THIS WHAT YOU
MEAN?

"The basic tool for the manipulation of
reality is the manipulation of words.
If you can control the meaning of words,
you can control the people who must
use the words."

— PHILIP K. DICK

"BOOK ONE SHEET"

A "BOOK ONE SHEET" is a resume for your book.
I've included an example of one of my own. I mocked
it up to present to Hudson News to try and establish
distribution (get them to buy my book from Ingram) to sell at
airports. They can be used to present and promote your book

anywhere, but are geared for retailers who already have access or an account with Ingram or buy from the various catalogs Ingram feeds. As a self-published author who tends to your own business affairs, you can work on print distribution this way, but not everyone does:

One sheets are used in all kinds of professions, as you'll see (or know). If you are a speaker you might have a *media one sheet,* for example, so this is not exclusive to books but all kinds of media.[71]

"ARC" or "Galley"

An "advance review copy" or "advance reader copy" or "galley" is simply a pre-publication copy of your book used to give to readers who will read and review your book for strengths and weaknesses, provide advance reviews for marketing, consider for purchase or sale, or given to potential guest writers when you invite them to write a foreword for you. These come into play in our "beta period," which we discuss in the Book Creation Cycle steps later in this book and even more in the next book, *The Book Creation Cycle.*

They can be in print or digital format.

I found an ARC for *The Tipping Point* by Malcom Gladwell in a Goodwill once and practically jumped up and down (not really). In addition to the badge on the cover that says "Advance Review Copy, Not for Sale," the back cover outlined the basics of the marketing campaign the publisher had planned—the $250,000 budget, the extent of the book tour, etc. Interesting.

"Marketing"

I wanted to define this because it depends, for you, on your goals and what type of author you are. For example, if you are

---

[71] In the entertainment industry, a one sheet (or one-sheet) is a single document that summarizes a product for publicity and sales. — https://en.wikipedia.org/wiki/One_sheet

a *legacy* or a *visionary* author and have one book, you might not even need a website. If you'd like to become a full-time author, you definitely need a website and should also start an email list.

So, in cases, "marketing" can mean leveraging your book in ways to secure clients and speaking gigs, and for anyone who wishes to grow an author career it really means *assembling a tribe.* It's all case-by-case and a marketing plan for you as an author should also take into account your interests and available resources of time, budget, and energy.

"LAUNCH"

Like different types of publishers, we now have different types of launches, described as either hard, soft, and everything in-between. Your launch plan should take into account your goals, resources, and any interest in making one or all of the different types of best seller lists.

- A **hard launch** has a definite date and scheduled events, perhaps months of marketing building up to that day, then "stacked" campaigns and ads and appearances from Tuesday through Sunday of "launch week," maybe even a book tour. The goal of all this time, effort, and resource for self-published authors is typically sales, reviews, and rank. For traditional publishers historically, they are testing to see if your book will "pay out," or make enough through your launch *week* to make back all that was *advanced* to you and then some, all taken as an indicator of likely future performance. I was told traditional publishers used to (and perhaps still do) guesstimate that how a book sells during launch week will predict what it's likely to sell each month thereafter. Many authors see the effort by their publisher completely drop after a less-than-successful launch, yet they are still bound by their contract.

- A *soft launch* might make a book available for sale in the quiet hours of the night with no hubbub whatsoever, the author/publisher having other goals and uses for their time, effort, and resources.

And there is of course everything in-between. All are fun and exciting, but understand that any launch is a *project*, and all projects involve *time, scope (effort), and budget.* The type of launch you choose should consider these things, be in line with your goals, and take into account *opportunity cost*, or asking, "What else could I be doing?" Those who launch soft, for example, have reasons to make a book live without cost or time involved, and then go about making their book *healthy, seasoned,* and *successful,* which we discussed in Part II, All Kinds of Books. For others, a *hard launch* might make their book healthy, especially if they already have a following.

"KINDLE"

I've added "Kindle" here because the meaning has recently changed. "Kindle" became so popular (being prevalent first) it became a household or generic name for ebooks, a la Kleenex, Velcro, ChapStick, and now, Zoom. Now it means more. Amazon disrupted the publishing industry with its *Kindle eBook* (as Amazon spells it). When Amazon decided to enter the print market, I understand they purchased a company called CreateSpace (as a strategic acquisition), which had its own website, so you'd publish your ebook with Kindle Direct Publishing (the "direct" part meaning it went straight to Amazon) and to get your paperback on Amazon you would publish through CreateSpace, an Amazon entity. (Publishing with IngramSpark also gets you on Amazon, but more on that later.)

A few years ago Amazon closed CreateSpace and moved that print platform under KDP (The transfer of titles was a bit wild for everyone!), which made sense and was cool because it's very simple and user-friendly to create one edition (ebook or paperback) in KDP and then with a few clicks (and different files) easily add the other (print or ebook) edition, with Amazon immediately understanding the editions went together on the retail site.

So today, "Kindle" still means "ebook," it's also an eReader, it stands for "Kindle Direct Publishing," which now includes print books, as well.

Amazon is currently beta-testing hardcover editions, and they've run with it in a pretty limited way so far, so there's now a *third* edition available in your book title's row on your Bookshelf in KDP. But at this writing KDP only offers *case laminate* as a hardcover binding option, and books have to be greater than 75 pages. There are also only a handful of available trim sizes in hardcover. Still in beta, and I'm surprised Amazon has not wanted or figured out how to offer case laminate in smaller books, as that would enter them into the children's book market. I expect they will, but who knows? Not all tests Amazon does turn into long-term offerings, such as drone delivery, for one.

But the modern author knows this, and that *tiempi cambi,* (times change).

"KEYWORDS"

A common misunderstanding is that "keyword" means a *single word* search engines (and think of Amazon as a search engine, YouTube as well) make note of so they (the algorithm, that is) can "index" your site/book/etc. and then suggest it when an applicable search is conducted by a user. This process of going over a site, book, or other product is called "crawling." When uploading your info and files to most book platforms they offer a chance to enter keywords, usually seven of them. But don't just guess at seven words! What you want—and it's a very important basic of your marketing, which we'll discuss much more—are seven *long-tail key terms,* which are simply several words strung together—call it a search *phrase.*

The most basic method of keyword research (there are more advanced methods) is easy to do. In fact, pro authors regularly test and update their keywords within KDP and IS and other platforms. Knowing what works can also help other marketing, even inform your subtitle, actually.

Here's an actual example of how I do this research in its most basic form:

1. Create a "brainstorm list" of keywords you think a shopper is likely to use when looking for a book like yours. I like to start with about ten of them. Let's say I'm looking for a book on cats and I write these first two terms down:

    a. Cat health

    b. Cat types...

2. Keep this list simple, because our next step is to slowly, letter-by-letter, type the brainstorm word into the Amazon search bar, with "Books" or "Kindle Store" selected as the department. Now, for this it's best to be signed out of Amazon so the results are not polluted by your own search history, and as you slowly type letter-by-letter, Amazon displays a drop-down list of popular search terms in an effort to anticipate and facilitate your search. Here's what Amazon suggests even before I've completed entering my test search term:

   a. When I complete typing "c-a-t" and hit the space bar, many popular search terms are suggested, two of them possibly relevant, being "cat book" and "cat training." I'd thought of neither, but they're both relevant and now I know, popular!

   b. I note these down until I have a list of about 14 and then choose what I think are the best seven, and *voila*.

Better methods of keyword research exist, such as running even a limited Amazon Ads campaign (for three months or more) and services like Kindlepreneur[72], as well as retaining an actual SEO expert, but the above is simple and so much better than throwing darts. In fact, by intelligent use of your keywords and categories, you can search and find different (and possibly the best) audiences for your book.

With an ongoing client of mine, she recently found homeschooling and "teen & young adult" to be a viable niche,

---

[72] https://kindlepreneur.com/

so we updated her categories and keywords and her rank shot straight up!

"BLURB"

Your "blurb" is your *marketing copy* or *book description*, that's all. Writing *copy* is specialized writing designed to get someone to take action. And it's highly valuable real estate on your online book pages, back cover, and marketing materials. It's one of the *marketing basics* that has to be "in" (good) before you even consider other promotion.

I like to follow a rough formula of starting a blurb with either a question that drives into whatever problem (in nonfiction) the reader likely has, and a question they will answer "yes" to, followed by a bit of expansion and then suggesting this book will solve that problem. *Do not make your book blurb a simple synopsis!* Bullet points (especially the "see page 84" kind) and great reviews are great as well, followed by a *call to action,* but be careful here as the rules seem to change regarding what Amazon, for one, considers an acceptable call to action. They will not allow, I don't believe, something like "BUY THIS BOOK TODAY!" for several reasons (all caps, and the aggressive nature), but I do think some sort of direction at the end is useful.

"METADATA"

Defining "metadata" this way is a bit of a misnomer, but it's useful. "Metadata" simply means "data outside" that which is found inside your book. In each client's project notes I have a section called "Metadata," which includes the info I'll need when uploading a book. Some of this includes, for handy reference (have all your stuff ready *before* you upload):

- Title

- Subtitle

- Author (name as it appears, and any pen name)

- Imprint (publishing name we've come up with)

- Blurb

- Bio

- Keywords

- Categories

- ISBNs

I also create a section or file that has "Author Data," and "Book Data" such as trim size, print and paper choices, and more, but these could all be lumped under "Metadata."

"KINDLE SELECT"

A word on exclusivity: Remember, Amazon likes to try and get your *eBook* exclusively. Most prominently with their

Kindle Select program, where you opt in to the program with your ebook for 90-day periods (and automatic renewals if you leave that little box checked). I generally recommend *maybe* trying Select in your first 90 days and evaluating whether to renew close to the end of that 90-day period, but I just as much discourage Select. The benefits are extremely weak, if you ask me. In Select, you can give your ebook away free for five of those 90 days, for example, but this is fairly ineffective in getting reviews, if that's your goal.

The exception is for romance and science fiction titles, where readers are voracious, gobble up books quickly, and often subscribe to Kindle Unlimited, where for a monthly fee they can read all the (participating) ebooks they want. Select makes your ebook available to Kindle Unlimited members, and as an author you get paid by the *number of pages* readers read. Amazon knows this electronically. Each month they divide the total sum received by subscribers, divide that by total pages read, and pay accordingly. I'm aware of authors in romance and sci fi who seem to make good livings this way, but in most cases you limit yourself with these exclusive arrangements.

"KINDLE UNLIMITED"

"Kindle Unlimited is a digital book subscription service that provides access to millions of ebooks, magazines, and audiobooks for a fixed fee every month.

—https://readingmiddlegrade.com/kindle-unlimited/

(I couldn't say it any better.)

"VANITY PUBLISHING"

I believe this was originally a term used to malign self-publishing by the traditional "elite," who were pissed off the commoners were raiding the pool, but it was probably coined earlier than my time and truly meant a book published not out of having something worthy to share but out of… vanity.

I'm happy to say now that perhaps the initial thrill and rush of everyone jumping in to try publishing a book has kind of passed, we see very little "vanity publishing" today and self-publishing has ascended to a true profession, dominated by professionals and worthy books. That said, I came across a true "vanity" title this last year and was surprised, which is a good sign, it seemed so rare. It was a "business card" book that over-celebrated a clearly privileged person's "struggle" and further, was highly materialistic in its "philosophy," followed by what we thought was not a serious and way-too-long and embarrassingly star-struck author bio.

I don't mean to gripe too much, though. The real point, perhaps, is that they *could have been more honest*—the pretentiousness was clear—and *your real motives come through your writing.*

And I know how it is, especially when you're starting out. We all want to succeed and the world puts great pressure on everyone. When I was a new real estate agent I got to show million-dollar properties for the first time to two gentlemen who flew in to buy in Florida. Well, I was still in home renovations and trying hard to make the leap to real estate agent, and all I had was an old work van. So, my broker lent me her brand-new BMW SUV. As I drove the two men around and we talked, they started to talk about their own cars—Lexus, Cadillac—and they asked me, "How do you like the BMW?"

"Yeah," I said, "It's okay I guess."

Oh, the beauty of understatement.

But I get it, we need to promote, and books are a powerful way to do it. But I learned even in real estate to tell the truth, and that your truth can be couched in positive ways. For example, "How many listings do you carry?" asked to a new agent would be answered…

"None. But if you sign tonight you'll be my *only* listing, which means I will live, eat, and breathe getting *your* house sold."

And it's the truth!

If you have to lie to make a sale maybe you should go home and rethink your life. Besides, when we lie most people can smell it. And more and more are learning to detect narcissists, so go about your book accordingly.

"LIGHTNING STRIKE"

Lightning happens, and we can do little to control it, it seems, but we can do *what we can* to attract it. A "lightning strike" is a sudden explosion of sales thanks to some unique event, and it's of course what most authors hope for. Lots of authors dream of getting on a national TV show, for example, to discuss their book, and while getting hit with lightning is an act of nature, we can at least "walk around with a metal pole." We can try to *attract* the lightning strike, but it's usually not as simple as walking out into a storm. To get on national media, start doing *local* media. Learn how to be a *great guest* (and there is such a thing as "media training" for this). And keep it going, you'll get there!

THIS IS MINUTEMAN TWO-THREE... GO!
MEMOIRS OF A HELICOPTER PILOT IN VIETNAM, IRAQ, AND AFGHANISTAN
WAYNE CHASSON

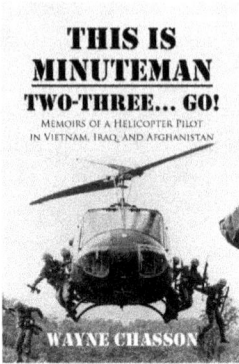

In Book 3 we'll discuss both organic and strategic growth for authors, and we'll talk about long-term as well as what Joanna Penn calls "spike marketing," those special usually one-time actions that *spike* sales, even if not then sustained or scaled. *Spike marketing* is akin to the lightning strike, but it does happen that standard actions create these opportunities as well. Author Erin Mahoney's *Girl Power* was chosen as a Read of the Month by a legit woman's magazine just by appearing as a new release in a woman's book category, for example. And *This is Minuteman: Two-Three... Go!: Memoirs of a Helicopter Pilot in Vietnam, Iraq, and Afghanistan* by Wayne Chasson seemed to take off *in the U.K.* almost as soon as we had it published, we had no idea why. But it was a bit of a lightning strike, but the popularity has continued! In fact at this writing his book has over 2,200 great reviews on Amazon[73]. And it couldn't have happened for a better narrative or a greater guy.

Phew! *Congrats!* I'll bet you now know more than most self-published authors! This has been a significant part of your "wax on, wax off" part of your training. We'll soon see what you can do with it. But take a break. Go walk on the beach. Hold your lover's hand. Hold your own hands. Contemplate the stars. Subscribe to my podcast. Consider coming to a weekend retreat with me in Cocoa Beach.

---

[73] https://amzn.to/44wh7hf

Next we'll finally learn the ten stages of a full and successful book project. Exciting! I get excited with each book project as they are born, develop, and come to life. So again, thanks for being here. Your voice, your ideas, should be included in the Great Library where they can benefit others (and you, of course).

And soon, they will be!

"First learn the meaning of what you say, and then speak."

— EPICTETUS

PART III

PLANNING, CREATING, & MARKETING BOOKS

"The general who wins a battle makes many calculations in his temple ere the battle is fought.

The general who loses a battle makes but few calculations beforehand.

Thus do many calculations lead to victory, and few calculations to defeat."

— SUN TZU, *THE ART OF WAR*

ALL THAT'S LEFT NOW is to... *start your book project,* if you haven't already. At last! We're going to do this and do it right. So many others have laid the groundwork and beaten the path to producing professional books so you don't have to reinvent the wheel, and all taken from experience in a variety of fields—from traditional publishing to real estate, project management, graphic design, marketing, public relations, and oh yeah—writing as *craft,* and much more. The framework, in my view, is the same, and might never change—create a worthy book, get it into the hands of people interested or get people interested (find or create a demand), accumulate a readership as we also continue to publish more books—or, if you're a credibility author, go about your new career as a speaker and/or high-paid consultant. Or support and disseminate your cause.

The terms, the methods, the technology, and catering to different genres might evolve but the framework stays the same, basically. For example, I've mentioned holding a *beta period*, and this seems to me to be the self-publisher's answer to the in-house developmental editor at traditional publishing houses, at least in part, and in fact, better, if you ask me. Beta periods have evolved and now fit the needs of self-published authors very well, yet so many either don't do them or don't know about them. So we have a list of best practices I've organized into ten stages, some that overlap and some that can (and should) go on concurrently.

I call it the *Book Creation Cycle.*

THE BOOK CREATION CYCLE

We've introduced this *cycle* earlier, and it's the entire focus and expanded on in *Book 2: The Book Creation Cycle,* but warrants mentioning here, because it is part and parcel of being a modern author, of course. Again, the ten stages are:

1. Planning

2. Writing

3. Editing

4. Design

5. Marketing

6. Production

7. Distribution

8. Pre-launch

9. Launch

10. Post-launch

This can be expressed as seven or twelve stages, but I finally settled on ten as hopefully a kind of ideal number. In fact the final decision for me on the number and order of stages came about through years of practice, as I have always sought to simplify and arrange a repeatable process for projects I worked on with clients, but it—the cycle—only got "finalized" in working on *this book series.*

And again, it's called a "cycle" because in a perfect world you *keep writing and publishing books.*

Let's quickly see what each stage involves, and what we have to look forward to in the next book:

1. Planning

We assess your goals, hopes, dreams, purposes, as well as time, budget, interests, and other available resources such as personal skills. We'll figure out if you will completely DIY or who and what you might hire. A rough or a precise timeline should be stated, all allowing a degree (or a lot) of flexibility to allow for both "life" and inspiration to intervene.

When you allow time for things to develop,
you are open to inspiration.

I learned that at 40 when I went back to college, and no longer crammed for every assignment at the last minute.

In the planning stage we also look ahead at what stages we might go through and when and how. In fact, when I do a free intro consult and it looks like an author-client and I will work together, the way I plan a project and share a project proposal is simply by taking these ten stages, laying them out, and filling them in according to what was discussed on that call.

In your initial planning we also discuss possibilities and the different types of *best seller lists,* and what it might look like if we go about seeking that, and how it influences your overall planning and strategy.

2. Writing

We figure out the best way *for you* of creating content, whether that's your notes, writing attempts, interviews, a full or partial draft you already have, or some combination.

*All of this is supposed to be just a tiny bit
beyond your current knowledge and skills
("challenging"), and with the guidance,
freedom, and flexibility to be one of the most
exciting things you'll ever do. That's how we
get your best book out of you, how you grow as
a person and/or professional, and how we
create something you are excited about and
proud of the rest of your life.*

Different authors have as many different best ways to create their content—some rigid, some loose, some yet undiscovered—but the stress in this stage is *the creation of content.*

A saying I saw once and love is this:

"I can't edit a blank page,
but I can edit a page of shit."
—UNKNOWN

So, in the writing stage, we create your content, more than we need, ideally. I'll state this again, if a bit differently:

*The way to write a great 50,000-word book is
to write a shitty 80,000-word book and edit
"the shit out of it."*

How content creation goes depends a lot on each author, and we often *discover* a best approach for you, and that often involves interviews, or transcribed dictation if DIY. There really are no rules. Remember my "top-down" (outline) method and my "spring" or "bottom up" method where we write from wherever the research (or in fiction imagination) takes us. When I started we'd ghostwrite books from as little as a two-word mandate (and I did, those being "clean water") or a 20,000-word book from 30,000 words of notes (and I did, for a doctor in the Philippines).

Great memories, lol.

And of course, we go much deeper into craft in *Book 2*.

3. EDITING

First and foremost, a case is made for *embracing editing*. I look to rock guitarists as analogous in how they write and edit solos, for example. David Gilmour (Pink Floyd) would solo, keep what he liked and ditch the rest, then do it again until he had stitched together something he loved.

That's *editing* and it *works*. And...

> *When you embrace and look forward to*
> *editing, it takes the pressure off your writing.*

In the editing stage we start on our *three types* of editing:

A.   Developmental editing

B.   Copy editing

C.   Proofreading

Development comes during or right after we you're your content, *copy editing* perhaps a little deeper when author and any collaborator feel they're "close" and again after any beta reader feedback (we might have more "development" at that point as well), and *proofreading* just before publishing, after interior design.

4. DESIGN

I design as soon as we start and as we go, and that's maybe a little backwards, but I'm sorry, I enjoy it. I love watching a book take shape and the fundamentals can be done early on, if you ask me. If your editor and designer are two different people, no worries, but for me, I like to jump into the development as well as the cover and interior design right away, as possible.

As soon as you have at least a probable cover or maybe even better, a number of covers to survey, you can start "marketing" at least in the sense of generating interest and excitement for your release. It also helps get the attention of likely beta readers, advance reviewers, maybe even a guest for a foreword, and maybe even *preorders.* But how concurrent things go depends on your timeline and if you have a team.

Your trim size and interior design matter, too, and will be influenced by your genre. And if this is a graphics-based book, there is no "too soon" for design.

5. MARKETING

If we have design started, we can actually start putting things before the public, as just discussed. It all depends on your particular case, of course. *There's much to learn about marketing books, as it's a specialized area of marketing.* And they say, "Half of all marketing works, we just don't know which half," which doesn't help, either. So start your marketing with "gambling money" and not much of it. A good *beta period* and experience will show what works for you and tell you what to focus on and scale. I'm now testing all kinds of "standard marketing" for authors with this and other books, as well as "strategic growth" principles for accelerated author growth, kind of the way the private equity dudes do it, for the third book in this series (so stick with me), but for now we can mention a few proven tactics:

- A short-form book proposal of about 1,500 words will be enlightening and inform your direction and effort, usually revealing things that are complete surprises.

- Many marketers rely on press releases. I wrote one once (although I am not per se a "copywriter") for an author-client, realizing media opportunities look for "what's news," and that news is *not* that we have new book. "What's news" is what's *in the news* (relevant) at that time. So I went to Google Trends[74]

---

[74] I also went to Google Trends when coming up with the title to this book, torn between "Smart Author" and "Modern Author." Mark Coker had that great podcast called "The Smart Author," which was a minus, and I thought "Modern Author" was more relevant and more precise, anyway. I compared the two terms on Google Trends and it was clear, there was more interest in the term "modern author."

and found the number one thing searched over the previous year was the iPhone. Well, this author wrote his book by dictating on his iPhone (he lost both hands previously in an accident), and voila, we had a news-worthy press release. *Fabulous book, by the way: The Sun Above the Clouds* by Paul Hebert[75].

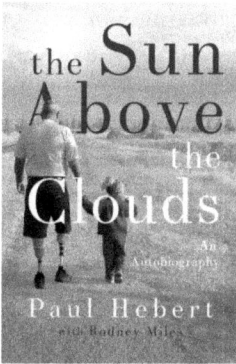

So, it's amazing what you will learn by diving into marketing, public relations, and more. That's what indies do, after all. Your marketing pro will tell you it's never too soon to start thinking or even working on your marketing, and it's true, but it depends on the purpose of the book project. You might not be in any rush to market and simply want to enjoy the process and go about things comfortably, or maybe the opposite is true and you're *writing to market,* basing your book on surveyed needs and wants.

A *beta period* can be terribly important in your marketing, too. While you might pull off getting feedback from beta

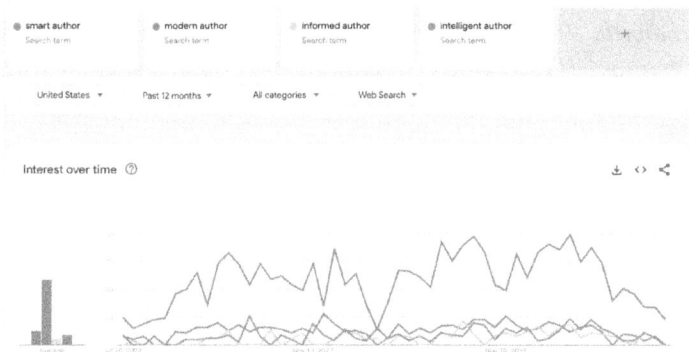

readers (usually free but there are paid beta readers) in as little as a week, holding a longer beta period from, say, one to six months, allows time to choose, start, then test marketing and ads, as well as build *infrastructure* like a website and funnel(s). All so we have proven, effective ad campaigns we can "stack" during launch day or launch week.

That applies to your book. Of course this time can also be spent developing and implementing marketing *you* and/or your business. And if you're doing a *hard launch* you'll want the lead-up time. Conversely, you can probably see now the appeal of a *soft launch,* with no fanfare, no commitments, saving all that time, energy, and resource for other things. I'm so busy I'm soft-launching *this book.* It's the first in a series, anyway, so I plan to buckle down on marketing more and more as the three volumes see daylight. But I did do a very crisp/short beta period, in which I got invaluable beta feedback, advance reviews, and a kick-ass Foreword—all in a couple weeks, really (maybe it bled into a month). But you see, by discussing all of these stages in your planning stage you can get clarity on a lot of things before you start moving forward, like lights on the highway ahead at night.

Otherwise, as a core of principles, based on my own experience and from watching hundreds of other authors, I have marketing broken down into four *tiers* across multiple *channels,* utilizing modern principles such as "funnels" and "bumps." (Don't worry, I'm just teasing you into sticking with me for Books 2 and 3.)

6. PRODUCTION

Notice, "production and distribution" are *before* your pre-launch period, and that's because we should already have (although it should be revisited in this stage) a *distribution strategy* mapped that affects the entire process and timeline, and we might want print copies for our pre-launch period. Otherwise, production is simply that stage where files are finalized according to platform specifications in preparation for upload and release. Part of that includes (although we'll have time to amend) formulation of your metadata, such as your bio, book blurb, categories, and keywords. This stage also includes, if not already taken care of:

- Copyright registration

- Obtaining a Library of Congress Control Number (LCCN)

- Purchase and registration of ISBNs

7. DISTRIBUTION

Distribution, for our purposes, is the uploading of files to the publishing platforms we've chosen (so they can be *distributed* to retail channels and made available for sale!). This is actually a *final step* of distribution, as again, our distribution strategy has by now been planned according to our goals. After successful uploads, files undergo a process unique but similar with each platform we choose to publish with. With a print book with Ingram, for example, as long as our files pass the initial computer verification upon upload, we then wait "up to 72 hours" for the *final* approval of files *by the platform* at which point Ingram supplies us a PDF *proof* to approve (or disapprove and make changes). Actual print proofs are also available. With KDP, if your paperback is approved by them within those same 72 hours, it simply goes live on Amazon.

With an audiobook, it's now standard with both ACX and FV to wait ten business days after initial approval of uploaded files for an audiobook to go live on Amazon via ACX or start to be distributed to various platforms with FV.

All of this can change, but you need to know what current wait times are if you are planning a launch and marketing, of course. You don't have live retail links until your book is live.

8. PRE-LAUNCH

This is that "beta period" I keep talking about, and a lot can be done in this period, of usually one to six months. I knew an old-time book publicist once who explained he preferred (in the old days of mainly traditional publishing) *one full year* from the *completed book* to work on publicly for the launch. The speed with which the world moves and the speed of digital publishing today seems to make that an anachronism, and handling beta-period opportunities can again be done in as little as a week and maybe as much as six months. Some of those opportunities include:

- Beta readers who give impressions and suggestions

- Advance reviews and endorsements

- Testing marketing and honing in on what works before/for launch day/week

- Building infrastructure like a website and funnel(s)

- Inviting a guest to write a foreword

- Planning launch, including any

    o Appearances

    o Parties

    o Ad campaigns (perhaps "stacked")

- Any best-seller strategy

I've found a good beta period has the added benefit of the *confidence* it gives an author. Think about it, up to now, you and any collaborator, your editor, your *alpha* (first) reader, your book designer, and perhaps your spouse are the only ones who might have seen your book, really. After just a handful of trusted beta readers and their feedback, we have test results! I find then pressing SUBMIT on your release is a whole lot less stressful and ideally, *exciting*—as it's supposed to be!

9. LAUNCH

Hard (with a specific, announced and promoted launch date/period) or soft (going live quietly in the night), this is when your book goes live. Launches and their purposes have changed a lot when it comes to self-publishing. No longer a critical test to see if a book and author "pay out," your launch strategy is something to be discussed and considered, as it's a project of its own, and the time, scope, and budget involved should yield results greater than the costs. One author might build up to a week of events and stacked ads, while another simply makes a book live with zero hubbub, and get back to work on other books in their series as part of a larger strategy. I've worked, of course, with both, and each has its place.

10. POST-LAUNCH

Once your book is live and your launch period over, there are things to do and make sure of, such as having a longer-term pricing strategy in place. Perhaps you're starting at a bit of a discount for early reviewers, family, friends, colleagues, or for whatever reason, but have an eye on a BookBub campaign and will need to go full retail price for a while. Maybe you are working on getting to 25+ reviews on Amazon before raising your price. Maybe you now price *high* to build value and credibility (altitude) and so that when you offer the book for free to potential clients, *they see value in it and jump on it.*

With one client as I write this, we soft-launched last October and are building infrastructure and a *net of lead magnets* (perma-free smaller books) in anticipation of his second in the series for early next year. Dionisios[76] *will be* a full-time author if he chooses. His writing and ideas are that good, but has a young family and a good day job, meantime.

On Amazon alone there are still steps to take *after* your launch, like refining your categories and claiming your books on Author Central.

And let's not forget about all the cool stuff we can do now that our book is live!

---

[76] www.DogsofCreation.com

So "post-launch" is *still* an important period, but the main thing I like to encourage at this point is now *your next book.* If more clients put out a book each year they'd be full-time or much closer to full-time by now, or at least have that option, more and more. That's regardless of why and how you plan to publish a book. Remember the formula:

List x List = Viability

And, a *series,* if possible, makes marketing and selling your books *so much easier.* One author at a roundtable once explained, "If I could go back and do things over, I'd complete the series before I did *any* marketing."

CONGRATULATIONS!

"An idea is anything that can change
how people see the world. If you can
conjure up a compelling idea in people's
minds, you have done something
wondrous. You have given them a gift of
incalculable value. In a very real sense, a
little piece of you has become
part of them."

— CHRIS ANDERSON,
HEAD OF TED (CONFERENCES)

YOU, NOW, ARE a MODERN AUTHOR, *congratulations!* As you have hopefully seen, as a self-published author you have *unprecedented* freedom, choices, opportunities, and control of your book, your business, and your destiny. You might find yourself answering questions of friends and colleagues moving forward, even more so than asking them. (But never stop asking questions, it makes you a king, *as-king.* There is power in words.)

BOOKS & PROJECTS
ARE SACRED

It's completely true that the process done well yields a *professional-quality book,* and often unexpected benefits of clarifying and codifying *your own expertise,* as I found in my very earliest projects with clients and still find to this day. And if yours is a bio or memoir, it often leads to unexpected *epiphanies and catharses* as well. This is why I'm excited to share what I've learned in my career including the Book Creation Cycle of best practices. I'm also excited to think you might now add *your story* to the Great Library.

I'm also excited to think you are now *protected* from outfits that see your book crudely and simply and purely as a "product" to be completed as fast as possible, or from outfits that stress the speed too much, as they might be cheating not only the process but you of the fruits of what can come from a healthy book *project...* unless of course, that's what you want. But the true modern author insists on *good books.*

And every book project is special.

When they're not, I'll hope the purveyors will peacefully move on to other, more opportune fields of making moolah. When the real estate bubble burst in Florida, I watched all the hairstylists, landscapers, attorneys, and others who had gotten into real estate sales for easy money (and it was) move on.

Again, it's that quote...

> "Only when the tide goes out do you discover who's been swimming naked."
>
> —WARREN BUFFETT

To me, it seemed like people were going back to their natural environments, and that was a good thing, to again occupy the *valuable* stations they had started out with, leaving those more dedicated and willing to put in the actual work to man the field of real estate. Like the end/resolution of perhaps my favorite movie of all time, *Raising Arizona,* when even the convicts realize they belong back in prison and go there, and all seems normal and natural again.

Through these last 13 years I've watched the opportunistic crowd swarm through publishing, just as they did with the real estate bubble. Perhaps we've come through a *publishing bubble*? The great news is, we are more and more left with caring, interested, capable professionals in the world of self-publishing today. I can list the companies that were here 13 years ago and other self-publishing consultants I've worked with and respect, and it's a beautiful thing. It raises the game for everyone as what we do—share ideas and expertise, share human stories and imagination, share visions of a better world—is part and parcel of publishing books. And we, as the indies, are the Eskimos, intimately familiar with such a sacred process and product, as we add to the Great Library for everyone's benefit.

Today, self-publishing is a profession.

This does not mean a book can't be done quickly—it can, and it can still be done well with all the fruits of the process if you know what you're doing. That's the ideal, anyway, and *shouldn't we be led by an ideal vision of what can be?*

When you master a subject you start to have *judgement* in that subject. It might take 10,000 hours, but with guidance and good information, those hours are more efficient and fruitful.

So, again, *congratulations, Modern Author!*

I now capitalize that term because it now applies to a specific title, *yours.*

YOUR JOURNEY
IS SACRED

So many miles I've walked
So many rivers I've crossed
So many battles I've lost
Make me who I am today
And when tomorrow it comes
There'll be a brand new sun
This song is not over
It's just begun

— STICK FIGURE, "Fire on the Horizon"
from the album *Set in Stone*

While we each have our own reasons for writing and publishing a book or books, before we part for now, maybe a story of my own will encourage you to *do it* if this has been on the back burner for a while, encourage you to embrace mistakes, and encourage you to perhaps focus on what really matters to you.

The hero's journey is of course, filled with challenges and triumphs. We win from a healthy process, and when seen in the right light, we might win even more from our mistakes and losses. What did I win from this process, from writing *this book?* We talked about the ah-has that often come along with creating a book, and I had a few really nice ones working on this first book in the planned trilogy. For one, I had to finally streamline my process and organize it into stages. I had realizations about the process, like with *writing to market*, for example, and how it moves a few steps around, but still works.

But the big one happened just today, while I was editing this. I started writing this book with a long-standing kind of defensive position that, perhaps even rightly, insisted, "Self-publishing is something to be proud of." True enough, and it makes sense, because I came up in what might be the early days, when self-publishing was often attacked, and more mediocre books were being produced. But as I was editing and revising, it flowed right out of me:

Self-publishing is a profession.

How great! Of course it is! I was able to let go of the now-inferior idea of simply insisting on *being proud of it*. I feel like someone younger might look at me (maybe my daughter) strangely and say, "Well of course it is. Duh!" But I got to watch it—the industry—get there.

So we learn and develop from a healthy process, our wins are steps up in awareness, and with a patient eye we learn and grow from our mistakes.

A few years before I was a writer, just as my real estate office failed (and had it not, I might never have finally gotten into "the arts") I needed cash and was invited by a good friend to start up a sales business traveling around the Southeast United States. In preparation to leave from Florida, I had purchased an empty, used U-Haul box truck I'd need for the business and I was bringing my Honda Shadow motorcycle. The plan was to drive it up the little ramp the truck had, strap her in, and have it with me in my travels.

But I had never driven the bike into a truck, not yet, and that was next. My wife and I pulled into the driveway next to the truck and had a little argument (over something, not sure what) and in frustration I said, "That's it, I'm getting that bike in there right now."

"Do it slow," she warned.

"I'll get it in there," I said. I stomped around, opened the back doors to the truck, pulled out and set the aluminum ramp, got on my bike, started it, aimed it up the ramp, and in my mind calculated *I'd need some speed* to not fall sideways, enough speed to slide right up the ramp, stopping smoothly right in the center of the box, something I'd been putting off, and with all the confidence my angry energy afforded at the moment, twisted back on the drive handle, and as soon as I was in motion I knew I'd made a terrible mistake.

More balls than brains, most of my life.

The memory is clear but the visual I have is a smear. I glided up the ramp and felt the bike fishtail, but it was too late. In a futile attempt to get her under control, I swerved right up onto the *smooth, aluminum floor*, and the back of the bike slammed into the right wall, crushing my tender foot between the motor and a wood strip along the base of the wall (for strapping). The bike stopped and I fell to the left, trapped under the weight of the motorcycle.

I yelled one long, sustained expletive, I guess to try and block out the enormous pain coming from my newly-crushed right foot.

My wife and daughter appeared in the box doorway, then the landscaper who jumped off his rider-mower from across the street appeared, pulled me from the wreck, and carried me like a bride into the house where he laid me down. My loved ones brought ice, looks of concern, and suppressed laughter.

In a few days, I drove, accelerating and braking *with my left foot* from Florida to Birmingham, Alabama, with my heavily-wrapped right foot raised and stretched into the seat next to me.

And from that point on, I *respected* that bike, riding it, and the road, *gratefully*. I loved riding that bike, a lot, and it seemed I had gotten off easy. I'd learned how to enjoy riding it without being an idiot. "My motorcycle foot" now reminds me how lucky we are if we can learn large lessons from small failures. It could have been so much worse.

I don't know about you, but looking back, I have learned so much more form failure than success. The close calls make me grateful, and I look for the lessons in them. And if we're *really* smart, we learn from *others' crushed motorcycle feet*.

I had another invaluable lesson even earlier on, when I decided to work a weekend and skip my wife's best friend's wedding. I made very little money, earned the (temporary) dislike of my mother-in-law, and still, of course regret missing the *life event*, but what I learned was so much more valuable.

> *Life, it seems, is a constant*
> *evaluation of opportunity cost.*

These are the things that have made me "The Book Dude," and not vicious and ambitious. And in my heart, mind, and soul, *I am happy. What I do is fulfilling. It helps people and it helps me.*

As a self-published Modern Author, you can take much of your life into your own hands.

Check this out—Nurse James Pickering with Hospice wrote this remarkable article detailing the top five regrets people make on their deathbeds:

1. I wish I'd had the courage to live a life true to myself, not the life others expected of me...

197

2. I wish I didn't work so hard. This came from every male patient that I nursed. They missed their children's youth and their partner's companionship…

3. I wish I'd had the courage to express my feelings.

4. I wish I had stayed in touch with my friends.

5. I wish that I had let myself be happier.

    Life is a choice. It is YOUR life. Choose consciously, choose wisely, choose honestly. Choose happiness.[77]

And funny, just as I sit down to write this Conclusion, I happen to be reading *Breakfast with Seneca: A Stoic Guide to the Art of Living* by David Fideler, who writes:

> "… the preoccupied mind of a constant workaholic takes in nothing deeply. By constantly focusing on how to reach higher levels of status or wealth *in the future,* preoccupied minds can't fully enjoy the present moment."

---

[77] https://www.oldcolonyhospice.org/blog/bid/101702/nurse-reveals-the-top-five-regrets-people-make-on-their-deathbed

And remarkable enough, from Seneca himself about 2,000 years ago:

> "But life is very brief and anxious for those
> who forget the past, neglect the present, and
> fear the future. When they reach life's end,
> the poor wretches realize, too late, that
> they've been busy for a long time
> doing nothing."
>
> —Seneca, *On the Shortness of Life 15.5–16.1*

But here you are, with all of this possibility in front of you. And now, the skills to share it with the world. All you need to do is *make time* for yourself. Slow it down just a bit, man! Remember the story of the two bulls, father and son?

"Hey Dad, let's run down the hill and <<mate with>> a cow!"

"Let's walk down, son, and <<mate with>> them all."

Or, as Seneca says (because we really don't need "mate with them all," yet the bull story has a point):

> "Of all people, only those who find time for
> philosophy are really at leisure—they alone
> really live. For not only do they guard over
> their own lifetimes, they add every age to
> their own. All the years that passed before
> them are added to their own."
>
> —Seneca, *On the Shortness of Life 14.1*

And how do we access the thinking of the past and present? How do we "add every age" to our own?

Usually, books!

Now, he figured all of this out and wrote these things *while Nero was trying to kill him!* But then maybe that's what it takes for us to really wake up, sometimes.

And I'm not just pointing out the obligation you have *to yourself,* I am saying this in regard to our *culture,* because it's completely clear to me now how much we ignore what's going on around us because we are debt slaves, workaholics, set on fake happiness and fake materialistic goals, and before we know it, we're on our deathbeds, regretting "not having had the courage…"

But for you it's not too late.

And now, you're a Modern Author. There's actually a bit of responsibility in that. You can do things other people don't know how to do in the realm of *ideas.* Use that to boom your business, yes! Use that to memorialize your life, yes! Use that to entertain and educate children. Use that to create new worlds for others to enjoy, yes! But use it for good! And let it—your ability to self-publish—perhaps even start to *set you free.* Have an exit plan from your cubicle. Make time—Henry Rollins (hardcore rock musician) said to an interviewer once (paraphrased), "You don't find time, you make it." So, make it! Make time to see what the problem with that unhappy child in your neighborhood is, and for God's sake, what your City Council has been up to, because they are spending your town into debt, right now.

Most of us are really good people, but we've gotten too comfortable and let "others" take care of things, while they enrich themselves at our expense.

I do think there is a Great Awakening going on, and you will either *start asking questions,* because luckily, that's the simple first step, and be a part of it, or you will possibly regret ignoring the history going on all around you. But now you have one more valuable skillset to add your voice with, and…

You are a special human.

Remember, a person *is* a story. What's yours? And just as much, the people in and outside your sphere, they're *people.* They're three-dimensional and almost always have surprising stories, if only asked. Just learn about and watch out for the sharks, because they're out there, too. People *are* waking up today, and the Internet and books are a big part of it. Sunlight is a cure, not a curse. As a person with ideas, with expertise, with a heart and a mind, and with the ability to self-publish, you have a *power.*

With this and the other books in the series, I plan to help you use it.

GO ALL-IN

As a Modern Author, despite all the crap going on in the world and all the unique challenges, we live in the Age of Transparency, which you can prove for yourself. But what does that have to do with a book on self-publishing?

Everything.

If not the independents who find the courage to start important conversations, whatever your bent, then who? If not the masters of putting out ideas who will be courageously candid, then who? We're in a unique position, and we need to set the tone of transparency and honesty in all we do with books. In fact, that's not just Kum Ba Yah, that's tip-of-spear marketing, because frankly, people have had enough bullshit.

And I'm not talking about just your spiritual or political beliefs. I'm talking about the aspiring thought leaders in business who praise every billionaire. How do you know Richard Branson, Bill Gates, and others got where they are because they're "pioneers" or "brilliant business minds?" Too many get fame and wealth by compromising behind closed doors, and by holding them up based on their prestige or wealth alone is a disservice and a bad example in so many ways.

An old friend was about to give a presentation to a small group and just before she went on she related to the organizer how when she originally moved to the area she and her family were black-balled, they were made unwelcome (for whatever reason) and pushed to leave. Her cat was actually *killed*.

"Say that!" said the organizer.

"What?"

"Say that. Most of these women here have been through that and worse. It will be a strong way to engage with them and they will more likely relate with you."

It worked, she told me. It was a surprise to her, and it was amazing. I encourage you to be brave and consider the big picture of what you do. You might be a CEO or a clerk, young or old, but it's honesty the world needs right now, and transparency, and we're just the ones to do it.

Bad things continue when they are not exposed.

And now that you are a Modern Author and know the Book Creation Cycle, you are among the few who know self-publishing best practices. You even know what a *great book* is. String a line from here to there and make a great book, or at least a *good* one. I hope it makes penning that first draft easier and the rest of the process possible, and we all enjoy better books. If it should be done, it should be done well. I hope it makes it more fun. I hope this gets you primed for the challenge before you and for lots of ah-has. And I hope you get good at it.

Watching figure-skating couples in a Winter Olympics, there was a clear difference between the couples who had their attention on the highly technical and dangerous aspects of their performance, and those who had all of that down-pat and could focus on their *art*. I'd love to get you closer to focusing on *your art* and *your message*.

And I'd love to read it, by the way.

Remember, you don't need to hold back in your book. We've seen that if you do, the reviews will kill you. But if you put it all out there, people will pay you to say what's in your book! And how else do we fill our minds and hearts of we don't empty them out once in a while?

Send me a picture when you do finally rip open that cardboard box to reveal your book, or of you giving a book signing, or you on stage speaking, or your grandchild reading the kid's book you just published. Please. Then crack a bottle of champagne or rum and celebrate (if you drink).

And of course, join me on my podcast.

A GOLDEN AGE OF BOOKS

In a great movie called *North Shore,* the younger surfer is out in the water with the older surfer, who has taken the young outsider under his wing. They are sitting, floating on their boards, looking around. The younger comments to the older about the waves to come that he sees.

"Where do you want to be?" asks the older, and the younger looks, then swims off.

There has never been a more exciting time to write than *now*, nor so many opportunities that come with it.

Where do you want to be?

People revere authors. I was watching a retired Army general in an interview and it made me laugh, actually, because at the bottom of the screen it said:

GEN. <<so and so>>
AUTHOR, U.S. ARMY RETIRED

It listed "author" even before his career in the U.S. Army!

I'm sure he encountered bigger challenges as a general than as an author, and I get it—he's there promoting his book, but *wow*. It does show how high we hold "authors."

So the altitude you can enjoy as an author is very real. And with self-publishing available to anyone at very low cost or even for free, and with the multitude of ways we now read and enjoy books, I really see that we're on the brink or perhaps already into a Golden Age of Books. And you're now a part of that. Maybe the hardest part of self-publishing is that it can be so "all alone," and rely so much on simply *you,* but there are easy ways to create accountability or to make the time each day or week for research and writing. And I hope I've allayed your fears of shitty writing, because if you embrace editing— by you or others—there's cause for writing freely, and without fear.

More books than ever before could mean more authors than ever before. In the next two books in this series, we'll work out how you as an author stand out and thrive, doing something you love.

And there is so much left to write.

Self-publishing is about creativity and control, and it's about freedom.

So, happy publishing!

I wish I'd done it sooner.

About the Book Dude

Author photograph © Michael Roberts
In Focus Photography[78]

I'VE TALKED ENOUGH about me throughout this book, but in short, I love books, have learned the best practices of how to self-publish them, and gotten familiar over the years with the industry from my little space I occupy, here in Florida. I hope to share all of that now.

I am still a collaborator and consultant, and provide author services and other things as you can see on the next pages. *I'd love to hear about your publishing problems as well as your successes.*

Rod

---

[78] http://infocusphoto.us/

ACKNOWLEDGMENTS

DAWN, *I know no greater joy than to simply be with you, anytime, anywhere.* Your love, wisdom, patience, and endless support made all we do possible. You are the perfect wife, mother, lover, and friend. *I love you, always.*

Fallon, you're smarter and even more beautiful than you know. The love and compassion in your heart is a gift to the world, whether it knows it or not, yet.

Mom, you gave me the joy of *bibliophilia.*

Dad, you nudged and encouraged me to *write.*

And you've both been perfect parents, wonderful grandparents, and to this day offer wise counsel when it counts. Oh yeah, you're also my best friends. *Thank you!*

Lloyd, my (other) best friend, my career and my marriage might not have made it without you. You're the best friend anyone could have. You really are, brother. *Tangerine…*

I know I've done something right when I think of the family, friends, clients, and colleagues I have. As I started to get responses to seeking beta feedback I realized what a special *tribe* I/we have here. And so…

For a kick-ass Foreword, and for friendship and being a treasured colleague and in many ways a mentor for about as long as I've been doing this, *thank you* Lauren Clemett.

Special thanks to my generous beta readers: Branding genius, Lauren Clemett * Gifted fiction author, Dionisios Efkarpidis * Author of a remarkable memoir, Wayne Chasson * Friend, colleague, Inspiring Woman, Christina DeBusk * My adopted sister and lightworker, Michelle Hubbard * My Australian brother who kicked cancer's ass, Luke Amery * My brother in Christ who is about to share with the world, Robert Mulindwa * And perhaps the best people and the best deal in professional beta reviews, Sid and Pragna[79].

Thank you, self-publishing and author thought leaders David Gaughran, Joanna Penn, Derek Murphy, Tim Fox, and so many more. I support you out of both gratitude and hopes of helping others learn from you, just as I did and do. Thank you, colleagues, many mentioned in this book and let's add Kristen Wise and Maira Pedreira, my brilliant friends and self-publishing consultants at PRESStinely[80], and Rajat Dutta[81], content consultant, to that beautiful list. You have braved the formative period of self-publishing and make it a proud profession every day.

And *my beautiful, amazing, awesome, fascinating clients.*
You have taught me all I know.

Thank you.

---

[79] https://www.fiverr.com/sidharthhj
[80] https://www.presstinely.com/
[81] https://www.upwork.com/o/companies/~016404be5bdc7f3336/

PRAISE FOR
RODNEY MILES,
THE BOOK DUDE

"Would never have made it this far, wrestled through all the emotion, or believed I could do it without your input. I'm grateful to know you, and thanks."

—Douglas Scott, Author, *Forged by Fire*

"After recently publishing a poetry book, I can honestly say that I couldn't have gotten the job done without Rodney Miles. He helped me tweak the book to perfection and stayed patient and professional every step along the way. I would recommend him to anyone who is looking for a kind, intelligent, resourceful and accomplished publisher and/or business partner. My experience with him was a fantastic one, and I will definitely be working with him again in the future."

—Kristin J. Thompson, Author, *Into Blue*

"Mr. Miles, a professional writer and editor who has been the driving force behind hundreds of business books says it's true that someone who writes a book on a subject is viewed as an expert, but warns that it can negatively reflect on your personal brand if your book is poorly written. Rodney suggests writing a business book is a great way to open doors to speaking opportunities and media coverage, but many new authors are totally unfamiliar with the details and work required. Rodney highlights that most of the people he works with are 'perhaps at the busiest time of their lives' and this is, in his opinion 'often the right time to generate a book. When you are busy, your mind is creative, you are on the edge of genius and in the zone of productivity.'"

—LAUREN CLEMETT, AUTHOR,
YOUR BRAND TRUE NORTH

"OMG!!! OMG!!! OMG!!! I saw the book covers last night and was too excited and teary and amazed to respond. They came out even better than I imagined possible... Thank you so much Rod . . . I can't even describe my feelings right now."

—REVEREND MICHELLE HUBBARD,
AUTHOR, *SCARED AND SACRED*

"Rodney is a great professional with incredible expertise in the publishing business."

—JONI WILSON, EDITOR

"He's a wonderful professional and a class act."

—TODD SIMPSON, SIMPSON CREATIVE

"We are still all high and sooo proud of the book and are really seeing how much of a difference it is to have a published book. It has given new life to all our other projects. You are so awesome. Thank you for being so positive and supportive all through this long journey."

—SILJE TUXEN, AUTHOR, *THE TUXEN METHOD*

"They look so good I could cry. Every aspect passes final inspection and are ready for upload. I couldn't have asked for a better product. For that, I thank you Rodney a thousand times over."

—NICHOLAS WUDTKE, AUTHOR,
BLACK NEEDLE SERIES

"Hi Rod, thank you for all your wisdom and great knowledge and experience, you made a big job look easy. Writing the book was great, and you did great work on the editing. You made the book look great. I had a book signing in my home town and sold 100 books and we gave a presentation they loved. Thanks Rodney for making the book a great read. You are also an honest person and it was a great project, one I had been thinking of doing for a long time. Thanks my friend! Best to you and your wife."

—PAUL HEBERT, AUTHOR,
THE SUN ABOVE THE CLOUDS

"Oh yay! It was actually a really emotional process for me, Rod! I haven't thought so much about my life's journey in a very long time. It was a good reminder of what I've overcome! Thank you for a most incredible self-healing experience!"

—DENISE DUNCAN, FEATURED AUTHOR,
INSPIRING WOMEN TODAY, VOLUME 1

"Thank you Rodney!!! This book has quickly become a reality thanks to all your assistance. Well done!"

—GRETE CHRISTOFFERSEN, AUTHOR,
LEADERSHIP SNAPSHOTS

"I have had the privilege of working alongside many professionals and mentors throughout my business journey and I must say that working with Rodney as my book editor and designer has been one of the highlights for me. Rodney is not only brilliant at his craft, he is an incredible human being who gives from the heart and truly cares deeply for his clients and their positive outcome. In fact, he feels more like a friend after the many conversations we've shared and I feel grateful that our paths crossed. As you can see, I'm a big fan and I've no doubt I'm not the only one that feels this way about you Rodney! Thank you so very much."

—AMANDA CLARKSON, AUTHOR,
FRUSTRATED TO FABULOUS

"Thank you, Rodney. Without you the book would never have materialized. You've opened a door for me through which many more books will come. Rodney certainly has a way of firing up your creative thinking muscles and getting the best out of your thinking. It's a sure-fire way to actually getting your message out there and I would like to thank Rodney again for the incredible service he provides."

—PHILL ASH, AUTHOR, *THE CHOICE*

"Working with Rodney has given me the tools and the courage to write multiple books. He has been the imperative accountability partner I've needed to complete projects. Writing can be hard but having Rodney to turn to, bounce ideas off, and get intelligent feedback has been life-changing for me. I've learned about how to launch, market, design, write, and all the ins and outs of publishing. I'm so grateful!"

—GRETCHEN STRAIT STEWART, AUTHOR, *JOY MANIFESTO* AND *SIMPLICITY*

"When we first talked about what I was doing I really did not expect for it to be as easy or for us to connect as quickly as we did, Rodney. . . The material I had needed to be reorganized and fleshed out. We worked together on that and we decided to release the books with an end in mind. . . you really helped me do that . . . you came up with illustrations that captured what it was like to actually use these principles, and I was thrilled with all of that."

—BETSY JORDAN, AUTHOR, *BULLSEYE!* AND *COACH!*

"It's been huge, and the coaches that I coach . . . the one who initially shoved me into putting this all together, he now wants to make sure when he has a new group of coaches that they have the book. Very exciting. Super excited. . . I looked forward every single time we got together to get another chapter or two out of my head and into a recording that could be transcribed and edited. . . I loved doing them. It was really awesome to have you as an audience and funny—I felt it was easy to put the book together. . . you made the whole process super easy to me."

—CYNTHIA FREEMAN, AUTHOR, *THE POWER OF DONE*

"I have been working on my book project with Rodney for some time now—absolutely love every minute of the ride."

—LUKE AMERY, AUTHOR, *GANBARU MINDSET*

"As soon as I started reading my chapter alone, I knew this book will make the list. It's very powerful because of your work. Great job! I never doubted your ability to make this a gem and you absolutely delivered it."

—Delina Fajardo, Author, *The Choice*

"You came strongly referred. I then found working with you an extremely positive and 'painless' experience. You're a true professional and you made my life very easy! And the final product is outstanding. We created a bestselling book and I am now a bestselling author. It's elevated me above my colleagues and competitors and my book has opened doors to speaking engagements both nationally in the U.S. and internationally. In fact I am just back from speaking with my book in Costa Rica, Rome, and so many other places. So thank you Rodney for your tireless and never-ending work and support! I could NOT have done it without you!"

—Dr. Joseph Rosado, Author,
Hope & Healing: The Case for Cannabis

"Loved this experience. Honestly the most amazing person to work with. No games, just hard work, honesty and skill is what Rodney has. I'm so honored to have gotten the opportunity to work with you for my first book."

—Madam Kitty Peterson, Author, *Kid Boss*

"I can honestly say I can't thank Rod enough for all he did for me and my book!! Without Rod help I would have been embarrassed had I submitted my manuscript as is."

—Wayne Chasson, Author,
This is Minuteman: Two-Three... Go!

"As a first time children book publisher, I was somewhat lost and needed direction. Rodney Miles Taber assisted me by answering ALL of my questions whether it was about formatting a book, printing, pricing, marketing, distribution etc. Additionally, he kept me organized by providing outlines, tasks, and instructions. He made it a point to assure I knew what to expect throughout this process and motivated me along the way. Once my book was published, he did not stop cheering me along. He continued to provide support and promotion. He still checks in on my progress. I am so grateful I found him and will utilize his skill and knowledge via consulting services whenever I am in doubt. He is an incredible person and professional!"

—KELLIE CARTE-SEARS, AUTHOR,
MOVING AWAY WILL BE OKAY

"Rodney is an excellent editor and designer. He was professional, responsive and a helpful with every aspect of the project. I will definitely be working with Rodney on the next phase of my project."

—AUTUMN RADLE, AUTHOR,
LILA GREY, LET GO OF THE DAY

"Rodney exceeded my expectations ABOVE and BEYOND anything I could have hoped for. He was extremely professional and truly cared about the work he was doing to help make my dream come true. His editing, book cover design, file creation, publishing/marketing knowledge, and MORE, was everything I needed. Thank you, Rodney!!"

—ASHLEE LEPPERT, AUTHOR,
THE HURRICANE WITHIN

"Rod is an absolutely amazing professional editor. I loved working with him on this project and will continue to work with him in the future."

—BADI EBRAHIMI, AUTHOR, *LITTLE BRIGHT STAR*

"Rodney could not have been any better! He went above and beyond in helping bring my true vision to completion. He is creative, timely, and a hard worker to the extreme. Rodney is an incredible communicator, he pays attention to details, and he helps you with aspects of your project you would never have thought about. I could not more highly recommend Rodney to anyone looking for the best of the best. If I ever have more work like this, I will know exactly who to come to first! Thank you Rodney!!! A+++++++++++++"

—TERA DENEUI, AUTHOR, *FIGHTING FOR FREEDOM: A 21-DAY JOURNEY TO FREEDOM AMIDST INJURY*

"Rodney has expertise in every field possible in the publishing industry. He has vision and brings your ideas to fruition. He is very patient and personable. He maintains his 'no worries' attitude. He listens and communicates exceptionally well. Rod is also the one-stop-shop. He does it all. He knows this industry inside and out. I needed a developer to help me upload files to Kindle Direct Publishing but what I got with Rodney was so much more. He has a plethora of wisdom and knowledge in every area of the publishing world. If you have a question, he will have an answer. He responds quickly and gives many details to help to make a decision. 5 stars isn't enough for Rodney."

—MICHELLE PROVOST, AUTHOR, *ABC'S OF HORSES* AND *ABC'S ON THE RANCH*

"Fantastic work—amazing communication, very fast. Quality is very high, I will work with Rodney again. He made changes for me above and beyond and worked in good faith throughout the project to make sure that my book came out looking great. He really cares about authors and their success."

—ANDREW CARPENTER, AUTHOR,
BLOOD SAGA SERIES

"Rodney, This is really beautiful, my friend. It feels so much to me how the book has wanted to feel from the start. Thank you. Thank you. I'm so excited. Love."

—MATT THIELEMAN, FOUNDER OF
GOLDEN BRISTLE AND AUTHOR, *THIS IS COACHING*

"Oh my God, I just briefly scanned the book, and I am so in love! You're nailing it! I can't thank you enough for making my vision come to reality."

—MISH BUSH, CELEBRITY MAKEUP ARTIST AND
AUTHOR, *A MAKEUP ARTIST IN YOUR POCKET*

Dɪ Pɪù!⁸²

START HERE, of course (website):
WWW.RODNEYMILES.COM

Go there, and buy the next book in *The Book Dude's Guide to Self-Publishing* series! Or the whole set! Even signed copy! Or other editions (ebook, paperback, hardcover, audiobook when available). Or have one (or the set) shipped to a friend!

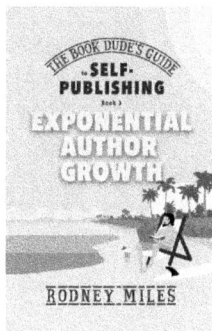

Also:

- Sign up for **emails** to find out about appearances and new releases.

- Read my **blog**, and read more about creating books.

- Visit my **bookstore** with my books, client books, and recommended books on craft and all things self-publishing.

You can also find about services such as:

- A *free* 20-minute **intro call**

- A paid 1-hour **private consultation** (with or without a customized project plan prepared for you)

- Buying blocks of hours for **author services**

- Attending a weekend self-publishing **mini-retreat** sort of mastermind thing in Cocoa Beach

- **Collaborating** on a full book project

- *And so much more!*

Check out my YouTube channel (@thebookdude): https://www.youtube.com/channel/UCSFY6AIOL-ObemaNzmINjBg

You can schedule a free intro call right here: https://calendly.com/rmiles, or just let me know what's good and we'll work it out. The Dude abides.

INSPIRING WOMEN TODAY

Please also check out my other passion project,
Inspiring Women Today.
… Maybe even nominate an inspiring woman
for the next book!

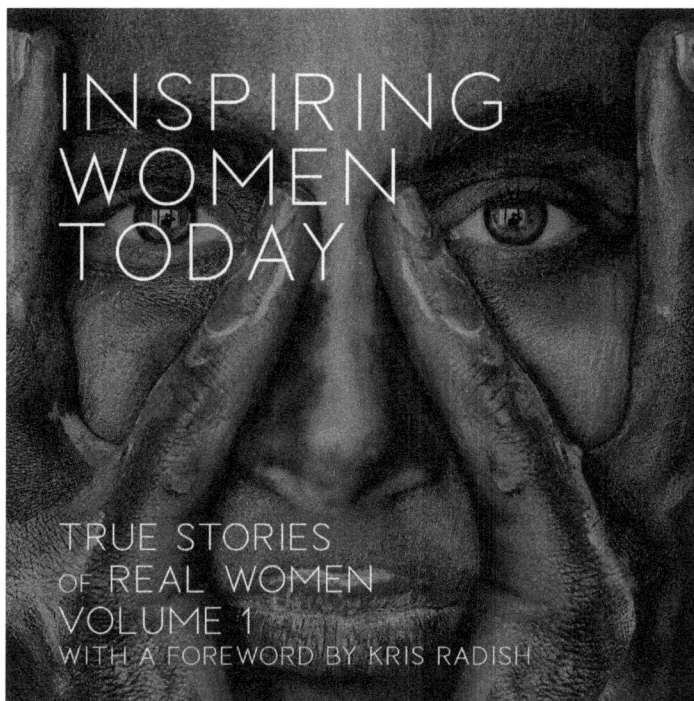

www.InspiringWomenToday.com

LIST OF ABBREVIATIONS

ACX: *Audiobook Creation Exchange*, online platform for uploading and distributing your audiobook to Amazon, Audible, and Apple Books.

D2D: *Draft2Digital,* online platform for uploading and distributing your ebook (although they are now promoting print/paperback as well) wide to many retailers with many options not available with KDP.

FV: *Findaway Voices*, online platform for uploading and distributing your audiobook wide/to many retailers.

IS: *IngramSpark,* the most established distribution network for print books, with an online platform for self-published authors to upload and distribute books (including ebooks).

ISBN: *International Standard Book Number,* simply, an identification number for easy reference (mostly by publishers and booksellers) assigned to each *edition* of a book. A single title/book with four *editions* (ebook, paperback, hardcover, audiobook) will need four ISBNs. Available for purchase in different ways, depending on your country (from Bowker in the U.S.). Many platforms now offer them free, but there are reasons to own your own.

KDP: *Kindle Direct Publishing,* the online platform/interface for uploading and distributing print and ebook editions to Amazon.

LCCN: *Library of Congress Control Number,* issued free upon application to the U.S. Library of Congress according to their numbering system for catalog records, in theory facilitating indexing by libraries when you seek to have them purchase your book and other identification purposes.

Lulu: *Not an abbreviation, it means "Lulu."* Online distribution platform for books and many other products.

RM: *Rodney Miles,* the most awesomest book guy to have around when you're creating your book!

www.ingramcontent.com/pod-product-compliance
Lightning Source LLC
Chambersburg PA
CBHW070103030426
42335CB00016B/1984